W9-AQL-109

◆

*Emily Dickinson,*
*Woman of Letters*

◆

# Emily Dickinson, Woman of Letters

*Poems and Centos from Lines in Emily Dickinson's Letters*

Selected, Arranged, and Augmented
by Lewis Turco

together with Essays on the Subject
by Various Hands

MIDDLEBURY COLLEGE LIBRARY

State University of New York Press

Published by
State University of New York Press, Albany

© 1993 State University of New York

All rights reserved

Printed in the United States of America

No part of this book may be used or reproduced
in any manner whatsoever without written permission
except in the case of brief quotations embodied in
critical articles and reviews.

For information, address the State University of New York Press,
State University Plaza, Albany, NY 12246

Production by Christine M. Lynch
Marketing by Dana E. Yanulavich

**Library of Congress Cataloging-in Publication Data**

Turco, Lewis.
    Emily Dickinson, woman of letters : poems and centos from lines in
    Emily Dickinson's letters / selected, arranged, and augmented by
    Lewis Turco, together with essays on the subject by various hands.
        p.    cm.
    Includes bibliographical references.
    ISBN 0-7914-1417-5 (cloth : alk. paper). — ISBN 0-7914-1418-3
    (pbk. : alk. paper)
    1. Dickinson, Emily, 1830-1886—Correspondence—Poetry. 2. Poets,
    American—Correspondence—History and criticism. 3. American
    letters—History and criticism. I. Dickinson, Emily, 1830-1886.
    Correspondence. Selections. II. Title.
    PS3570.U626E45  1993
    811'.4—dc20
    [B]                                                                    92-13837
                                                                              CIP

10 9 8 7 6 5 4 3 2 1

*This book is for*
*Jean, Melora, and Bertha,*
*and in memory of*
*May Laura,*
*the other women in my life*

# Contents

## Essays by Various Hands

# Acknowledgments

The author owes acknowledgment to the editors and publishers of the following journals and editions in which the poems gathered here first appeared: *Barnwood* for "The Gift," "An Old Tale," and "Passing"; *The Bloomsbury Review* for "Twilight Touches Amherst"; the poetry page of *The Buffalo Evening News* for "Brown Study" and "The Deep Stranger"; *The Centennial Review* for "The Amherst Fire," "Home," and "Nocturne"; *Chelsea* for "An Amherst Calendar" and "Passages"; *The English Record* for "Death"; *Escarpments* for "Crimson Children," "The Ear of Silence," "Epithalamion," and "The Harper of Stillness"; *The Galley Sail Review* for "The Clock"; *Hampden-Sydney Poetry Review* for "Among the Stones," "Late Fall," and "An Orator of Feather"; *Jeopardy* for "Late Summer"; *Kennesaw Review* for "Flowers in Season," "A Morning Picture," "Asea," and "Theme and Variation"; *The Kentucky Poetry Review* for "Housekeeping," "Morning Music," and "A Pearl Jail"; *Lake Effect* for "Company"; *Laurel Review* for "A Dream of Roses," "A New Year," and "Summer's Chariot"; *The Literary Review* for "The Winter Garden"; *The Mid-American Review* for "May, Merely"; *New CollAge Magazine* for "An Amherst Christmas" and "Epistle"; *The New Orleans Review* for "An Amherst Pastoral"; *The New York Quarterly* for "Fading Things"; *The Ontario Review* for "An Amherst Haiku," "Amherst Neighbors," "A Memoir of Evening," "The Mower," "Poetry," and "Scarlet Expectations"; *Poetry Northwest* for "A Dainty Sum"; *The Sewanee Review* for "The Cage," "Mansions of Mirage,"

"Marble Rooms," and "The Naked Eye"; *West Hills Review* for three of the "Four Small Songs"; *Whiskey Island Quarterly* (Cleveland State University) for "Cloth of Dreams," "The Miller's Tale," and "Sampler"; and *Williwaw* for "Adventure."

"Company" was issued as a Christmas card by Mathom Press Enterprises in 1984, "First Snow" as a Christmas card by Gray Heron Press in 1985, and "Fading Things" as a Christmas card by Mathom/Gray Heron in 1986, all illustrated by George O'Connell. The first section of "The Clock" originally appeared under the title "The Summer's Picture" in *A Folio of Maine Writers* from The Open Book of Portland in 1980.

"Poetry" was reprinted in *Visions and Revisions of American Poetry* (University of Arkansas Press, 1986) by Lewis Turco; "An Amherst Haiku," "A Dainty Sum," "First Snow," "The Naked Eye," and "Poetry" were reprinted in *The New Book of Forms: A Handbook of Poetics* by Lewis Turco (University Press of New England, 1986).

"Just God" originally appeared in the anthology *Light Year '87* edited by Robert Wallace (Cleveland: Bits Press), which also reprinted "Amherst Neighbors," "The Gift," and "The Naked Eye."

"The Cage" was reprinted in the *Anthology of Magazine Verse and Yearbook of American Poetry 1986* edited by Alan Pater (Beverly Hills, CA: Monitor Publishing Company).

"Delay" appeared originally as part of a tribute to the late John Ciardi in *The Dictionary of Literary Biography Yearbook: 1986* edited by Matt Brook (Detroit: Gale Research, 1987).

"Lamps" and "Small Victory" were first published in *Contemporary New England Poetry: A Sampler*, edited by Paul Ruffin (Texas Review Press, 1987), where they were credited to "Wesli Court."

One portion of the introduction was published as a "Letter to *Barnwood*" (Barnwood Press Cooperative, 1981), and as part of an article, "How Three Books Grew," in *The English Record* (New York State English Council, 1985). A second version titled "A Sampler of Hours" was published with "Winter Bouquet" as a comment on that poem in *Ecstatic Occasions,*

*Expedient Forms* edited by David Lehman (Macmillan Company, 1987); "The Gift" appeared as part of the essay in all these publications.

Another version of the entire introduction was published as "The Poetry of Emily Dickinson's Letters" in *The Public Poet: Five Lectures on the Art and Craft of Poetry* by Lewis Turco (Ashland Poetry Press of Ashland University, 1991). This version included "The Harper of Stillness," "Crimson Children," "The Ear of Silence," "Epithalamion," "Poetry," "The Gift," "A Dainty Sum," and "Winter Bouquet."

# Introduction

Everything in this book is a response to the letters of Emily Dickinson—not to her poems, her *letters*. My own response was to write a series of poems titled *A Sampler of Hours*, poems and centos from lines in the notes and epistles she sent to her friends and relatives, and the response of the critics included here has been to discuss, sometimes in a scholarly way, sometimes historically or critically or appreciatively—even lyrically—the letters in particular or in general. Some of the essays make the connection between the letters and Dickinson's poems. The critics did not know these poems and centos existed when they wrote their essays, nor did the author/editor of this book know the essays existed. The reader will find here insights and concerns that grew out of a contemporary burgeoning interest in the prose writings of one of the most important American poets, if not the greatest we have had to this point in our history, as I believe is the case.

If Dickinson's poems were usually dramatic works rather than egopoetic confessions, and they were, it was in her letters that the poet spoke most often in her own personal voice. During the winter of 1980 I read an essay by Van Wyk Brooks which quoted four lines from Emily Dickinson's letters: "The Moon rides like a girl through a topaz town"; "Tonight the Crimson Children are playing in the west"; "The lawn is full of south and the odors tangle, and I hear today for the first the river in the tree," and "Not what the stars have done, but what they are to do is what detains the sky" (Brooks, 260).

I was struck by the modernity of these prose expressions; their sounds and images seemed to me to have more of the feeling and flavor of modernity than even Dickinson's poems, or for that matter the lines of many and many a poem of the twentieth century. Immediately, I wrote four poems that included, and tried to live up to, the Dickinson lines I have quoted.

No doubt this was a foolhardy thing to do, but I had attempted the same sort of thing with Robert Burton's seventeenth-century tome, *The Anatomy of Melancholy*, and I produced a book of poems the whole title of which reads, *The Compleat Melancholick*, "A Sequence of Found, Composite, and Composed Poems, based largely upon Robert Burton's *The Anatomy of Melancholy*." I felt then, and I still feel, that my poems did little damage to Burton. The first four poems I wrote in a similar series based on Dickinson were "The Harper of Stillness," "Crimson Children," "The Ear of Silence," and "Epithalamion"—they will be found early on in the series.

People have asked me what I mean when I say that some of the imagery from her letters is particularly "modern," and that is a legitimate question. I mean by "modern" that the lines are written often in "abstract syntax," which was first identified and discussed by Donald Davie. The idea behind what I call "abstract syntax" and Davie calls "musical syntax" is the same idea as that which is behind "abstract art," which is to approach the condition of music in language or in painting.

Music is the most abstract of the arts in that there are no "meanings" attached to notes or musical phrases. There may be a kind of general *feeling* attached to some aspects of music; for instance, minor keys "feel" sad whereas major keys do not; fast music feels happy, but slow music feels moody. Aside from that sort of thing, no meanings inhere in music, yet we enjoy it because we can perceive musical structures and progressions, harmonies, dissonances, counterpoint, and so forth.

If painting, let's say, wants to approach the abstract condition of music, one must get rid of figures. If one is an abstract painter one gets rid of identifiable representations, of figures, in one's work. The same thing must be done in language, as well, if one is going to write using abstract syntax, and of course T. S. Eliot's *The Waste Land* is written partly in abstract syntax, Wallace Stevens is an abstract syntax poet, and one of the first Dickinson lines I read in the essay by Van Wyk Brooks that I mentioned was a line written in abstract syntax which I used in the poem titled "The Harper of Stillness": "The lawn is full of south / and the odours tangle, / and I hear today for the first / the river in the tree."

What does that *mean*? The syntax of the line does not come to a point where one can say, "Oh, that means this, that, or the other thing." It is an approach to music, and I think the line is stunningly beautiful. One of the other three is like that, too. The poem that I call "The Ear of Silence" starts with a sentence written in abstract syntax: "Not what the stars have done, / but what they are to do / is what detains the sky." So, two of the four Dickinson lines that Van Wyk Brooks quoted from her letters were sentences written in abstract syntax.

The point with most poems written in abstract syntax is that there *is* no meaning other than the poem itself. As Jenkins wrote,

> The vastness of the thought she wished to express defied, sometimes, the limits of her cryptic pen. She knew what she meant. It was all clear to her, but certainly after many years, and in the silence of those to whom the message was sent, it is difficult to catch the meaning of some of the notes even in my modest collection. I confess my inability to understand what is beneath this message sent to my mother in Pittsfield. What its occasion was or what gift, if any, it accompanied I do not now recall, if indeed I ever knew. She writes:
>
> "Dear Friend,
>> "Were the velocity of Affection as perceptible as its sanctity, Day and Night would be more Affecting" (Jenkins, 115-16).

What one is really doing with words when one employs abstract syntax is manipulating connotations, associations and overtones, and not primary meanings, denotations. Dickinson did not get those overtones into her poems as often as she got them into some of the lines from her letters.

The other kinds of syntax, according to Davie, are "subjective" syntax: sentences that express personal opinions, "I'm nobody! Who are you? / Are you nobody too? / Then there's a pair of us—don't tell!"; "objective" syntax, sentences that express actions: "The flowers have reached the eaves / and are heaving against the roof / which has begun to buckle—"; and "dramatic" syntax, as when Dickinson puts words into the mouth of a person who is dead: "I heard a fly buzz when I died." Those are the three traditional syntaxes.

Abstract syntax is really a twentieth-century phenomenon, except, of course, I am showing that it appeared in the work of Emily Dickinson in the nineteenth century. And it appeared in both her letters and her poems—in other words, in both her prose and her verse, which in itself is an unusual phenomenon because there is not a whole lot of abstract syntax prose in the world, although James Joyce's *Ulysses* and *Finnegan's Wake* may perhaps be examples.

In the twentieth century various writers use abstract syntax for various purposes. The major abstract poet of the twentieth century so far is Wallace Stevens. Oddly enough, he was a message poet. His message was that mankind had to get rid of romanticism, religion, and all that emotional baggage that we ought, as a race, to have cast aside by now. We ought to substitute for them an existential viewpoint which would allow us to get through life with dignity, without resorting to the crutches of tradition.

Now, Stevens could have said that in so many words, and in a way he did in some of his poems, but really what he did was to wrap around this idea some amazing tropical images when he was young and, when he was older, images of the arctic. It is often extremely difficult to get down beneath the imagery to the bedrock of statement, to the condition which he called, in his early poem "The Snowman," a "mind of winter." It takes a mind of winter for modern men and women to bear up under the weight of mortality and the perception of that mortality.

Stevens used abstract syntax because he had to in order to write the "larger poem for a larger audience" that he talked about and called for—the largest audience being, one supposes, all of the race of Man. Otherwise, it was just, write an essay and get it over with. But writing poems was how he proposed to get through life without the lush security blanket of religion wrapped around him. Do we suppose that Dickinson had a significantly different purpose in writing her poems?

What about her letters? Often Dickinson included poems in her letters, and in fact many of the poems that appear in her *Complete Poems* were culled from letters that were sent to her correspondents.

When I had finished the first four Dickinson-inspired pieces I sent them to a magazine at the State University of New York at Buffalo entitled *Escarpments* whose editor, Carol Sineni, accepted them immediately and published them under the title "A Suite for Emily" (Spring 1981). However, I was by no means satisfied with them myself, for I felt I had not assimilated Dickinson's tone and style, nor had I made my additions indistinguishable from her quotations. I went to the library and checked out Dickinson's *Letters*, hoping to find other lines I might quarry. Much later I was fortunate enough to find a copy I could purchase for my own library.

The images in Dickinson's verse are striking, but it seems to me that when she put tropes into her verse something about the process changed the quality of the images—perhaps she was merely not quite so self-conscious when she was writing letters.

By 1984 I had written sixty poems in a series I have titled *A Sampler of Hours: Poems and Centos from Lines in Emily Dickinson's Letters*. Some readers of these pieces, nearly all of which first appeared in the literary periodicals and various anthologies and books, wish to know which lines are Dickinson's and which are mine. At first I tried italicizing her words, as I had done with Burton, but that practice seemed to break up the poems badly, whereas in the Burton poems it actually seemed to help. As a result, some people have fallen into a guessing game almost automatically, which I deplore, but it *can* be amusing, to me at least, because the conjectures are generally wrong.

If they were not, I would have been unsuccessful in assimilating Dickinson's style, and the poems would be failures. Perhaps they are—readers will have to judge that for themselves. The subtitle of this book indicates that I have "selected, arranged, and augmented" Dickinson's lines. In the first four poems I simply used each of her quotations as the first stanza of a poem, breaking the passage at the ends of phrases—what William Carlos Williams called "the breath pause"—and writing subsequent stanzas in the syllabic line-lengths into which Dickinson's phrases happened to fall. For instance, the first stanza of "The Harper of Stillness" fell into the form of a quatrain, the lines of which happen to be 6-6-8 and 6 syllables long; thus, the succeeding stanzas are quatrains with the same syllable counts line for line.

At times I have done little more than select a complete passage from a particular letter and cast it into syllabic prosody; more often, I have taken lines from various letters and arranged them in some sort of order. Reasonably often I have augmented Dickinson's lines with my own. Some poems are almost entirely hers, others are more mine than hers, but "The Gift," a single couplet and the shortest poem in the series, may serve as an example of the method of composition I used most often—the first line is Dickinson's, the second is mine.

A poem that is made entirely from Dickinson's own lines culled from various parts of her letters is one I titled "Poetry." It is practically everything that Dickinson had to say about the art and craft of writing poetry. It is what might almost be called a "found" poem. A poem that is a true collaboration is a lyric titled "A Dainty Sum."

On one occasion, when I was giving a reading from these

poems in Portland, Oregon, I was accused by someone of "tampering with an American classic," but this is not so. I have touched none of the canon of that classic, the poems themselves; I have worked only with her letters, which few people read. If any of these poems work, then all I have done is bring to the attention of a modern audience a number of Emily Dickinson's beautiful and startling observations that would otherwise have remained buried in the bulk of her prose.

This, it seems to me, would be a shame. There is a real sense of her personality that comes through her writing. I mean, you feel as though you know her, as though she were your next-door neighbor, and you feel fortunate in the friendship. I have never met a person who had such a brilliantly wide-ranging mind, or such an ability to toss off, seemingly at random and on any occasion, images as arresting and colorful as any in American poetry, or to match in depth of perception and succinctness of expression the flowers of anyone's intellectual garden.

LEWIS TURCO
Oswego, New York

## References

Brooks Van Wyk. "Hawthorne in Salem, 2: Emily Dickinson," in *This Is My Best*, ed. Whit Burnett. Cleveland: World Pub. Co., 1942.

Burton, Robert. *The Anatomy of Melancholy*, ed. Dell and Jordan-Smith. New York: Tudor Pub. Co., 1927.

Davie, Donald. *Articulate Energy*. New York: Macmillan, 1958.

Dickinson, Emily. *Bolts of Melody: New Poems*, ed. Mabel Loomis Todd and Millicent Todd Bingham. New York: Harper & Bros., 1945.

———. *Complete Poems*, ed. Thomas H. Johnson. Cambridge: Harvard Univ. Press, 1951.

———. *Letters*, ed. Mabel Loomis Todd. New York: Harper & Bros., 1931.

———. *Poems, [First Series]*, ed. Mabel Loomis Todd and T. W. Higginson. Boston: Roberts Bros., 1890.

———. *Poems, Second Series*, ed. T. W. Higginson and Mabel Loomis Todd. Boston: Roberts Brothers, 1891.

———. *Poems, Third Series*, ed. Mabel Loomis Todd. Boston: Roberts Brothers, 1896.

Eliot, T. S. *The Waste Land and Other Poems*. London: Faber & Faber, 1940.

*Escarpments* 2 (Spring 1981).

Jenkins, MacGregor. *Emily Dickinson, Friend and Neighbor*. Boston: Little, Brown & Co., 1939.

Turco, Lewis. *The Compleat Melancholick*. Minneapolis: Bieler Press, 1985.

———. *The New Book of Forms: A Handbook of Poetics*. Hanover: Univ. Press of New England, 1986.

# A Sampler of Hours:
## Poems and Centos from Lines in Emily Dickinson's Letters

♦

## Cloth of Dreams

In what shall I be clothed today?
      Sack cloth and ashes?
   Or has that feeling died—
   Shall I wear crepe for it?

Perhaps I ought to choose a chintz
      To prance about in,
   or dolor of linen
   in a nice winding sheet,

such as Emerson's Aunt Mary
      Moody chose to wear
   on social occasions
   in her native Concord.

But no, this is Amherst. We wear
      no shrouds in this town.
   Love, like the cloth of dreams,
   cheapens other fabrics.

## The Harper of Stillness

The lawn is full of south
and the odors tangle,
and I hear today for the first
the river in the tree.

The cricket in the root
has found a note to cast
upon the pool of eventide,
of shadow welling from

a coast of pines. Swiftly
now he comes, the harper
of stillness, lifting up his strings
to net the western fire

shoaling the upper limbs,
the roofs of our houses
swept by a wave of daylight lost
in the depths of summer.

## Crimson Children

Tonight the crimson children
    are playing in the west.
They do not hear the stars call
    down the burning sky
that time has passed, is passing
    under clouds afire,
tumultuous with ash.

## The Ear of Silence

Not what the stars have done,
but what they are to do
is what detains the sky,

keeps it from failing us
now when the children sleep
in rooms of dream's keeping.

What does darkness confide
in the ear of silence,
vessel of the hollows?—

echo of a sunken
bell ranging the far fields
of light, the well of chimes

that takes us awake now
in our waiting for night
and the starlight falling.

## Epithalamion

The moon rides like a girl
   through a topaz town,

her steed the beast of air,
   the mount of the wind.

We see her riding there
   where the desert knocks

against the horizon,
   cactus burning like

silver on seas of ore.
   But our doors are shut—

they are studded and barred,
   and if we are still

she will pass in our streets
   blind to our whispers,

deaf to our lingering.
   The sand will take her,

this girl who comes riding,
   this bride of the night.

## The Mower

The mower is tuning his scythe
in the long meadow
looking for a voice.

## A Memoir of Evening

The book is fair and lonely,
like a memoir of evening—

sunlight spills from its pages,
the note of a dusky bird;
a glass stands on the table,
    and a bowl of fruit,

but these are no miracles,
companions of the twilight.
Something is among the crickets
still as the sky that closes—

not one word comes back to me
    from that silent West.

## Scarlet Expectations

Second of March and the crow
and snow high as the spire,
and scarlet expectations
    of things that never come,
    because forever here:

the cardinal in carmine
on the sacrament of snow
whistles to the wind his fruitful prayer;

the nut-hatch and chickadee
confess their want of winter
alms in the cathedral pine:
    New England has none to spare,
    you think, in its season?

Perhaps you think I *have* no bird,
and this is rhetoric—
pray . . . what is *that* upon the cherry tree?

## Mansions of Mirage

I live in mansions of mirage
       where seeming turns to Be.
The leaves of summer near the winter glass
        etch themselves in frost;
the busts in the conservatory nod

    in shadow—I am not less wise
       for that marble story.
The many households clad in black attire
       are where others live.
I come in flakes . . . the bright inhabitants

    of the white home where strange blooms
       arise on many stalks
and trees receive their tenants. On the stair
       that falls like water
I meet my voice in amber speaking of

    the undertow of the organ—
       a similar mirage
of thought, a woe of ecstasy in white:
       she will pirouette
in a paper room, not in the parlor

    among the guests; they do not know
       the blood is more gaudy
than the breath but cannot dance as well. I
       will raise the lid to
my box of phantoms. There I will not find

    among my souvenirs in season one
       to startle, to cry
a cold yet parched alarm that chills and sears.

## A Dainty Sum

One is a dainty sum!
One bird, one cage, one flight;
one song in those far woods

where mandrake likes to dream,
where dragonfly patrols
its image in the stream;

one song out of the limb
of juniper or fir
moving across the field

where primrose tries to snare
the note of solitude,
the message from the air.

## Marble Rooms

The rooms were marble
    even to the flies
that trod the noses of those stony folk

    who stood in the hall,
        their words like agates
rolling from their lips, clicking and skirling.

    What was it they said,
        those heroic folk?
When they turned an ear, did the voice crack,

    the fair brow take a stain?
        The vine came rapping
at the windowpane, the sunlight coiled

    round about the pillars,
        rubbed the ridges smooth.
The shadows hid beneath the furniture

    like creatures caught in time,
        lichens in the dust;
the mortar turned to powder on the floor.

## An Old Tale

I hear the wind blow the wide way
in the orchard, snaring itself
    in the April limbs,

telling its story to the lymph
rising to Spring. It is an old
    tale, forever fresh,

and in it one can nearly hear,
*diminuendo*, the first lines
    of Autumn's legend:

the bloom and the fading away,
· the sere blossom, the petal pressed
    between the ancient leaves.

## Morning Music

Where is the morning music,
    the song played at the sill?
    I cannot remember

how it went in its feathers,
    only that it went well
    preening and disporting

against the window casement.
    The garden enjoyed it,
    I recollect, nodding

and nodding. The melody
    went this way and went that
    to the twigs tapping glass.

One day I will recall how
    only the pines sang tunes, now
    the birds are absent.

## Twilight Touches Amherst

Now the grass is glass
and the meadow stucco.
Twilight touches Amherst

with his yellow glove.
Do you recall Summer
with its meadows in bloom,

gardens full of light
settling in bright petals
upon the flower stalks?

Nothing has been changed
but the season—all things
have been changed but the mind,

which is change itself.
When will you come again
to see the springtime fall?

Miss me sometimes—not
on most occasions, but
the seldoms of the mind.

## The Gift

A one-armed man conveyed the flowers.
I gave him half a smile.

### Home

The forests are at home—
the mountains intimate at night
and arrogant at noon.

I am at home as well—
there are meadows in my parlor,
and in the bedrooms, vales.

### Sampler

Many an angel, with its needle,
    toils beneath the snow
making a sampler of hours
    that fades with the sun

just as the snowfall fades to reveal
    a green alphabet
written in the script of flowers
    bordered in lilac:

the arbutus is a rosy boast
    adrift in morning;
zinnia, an ochre brag
    along the far fence.

What is there between them but waiting
    for the sky to rise,
lifted by the seraphim
    who ply their stitching?

## The Cage

This morning sang at the windowpane
and asked to come in—I let it
fly in the halls a little;

it went sweeping out when you arrived.
The sun perched on the roof listening
to the gift of tongues you bore,

but after a short while it felt faint.
A colloquium of shadows
fell to discussion of it.

After you went, a low wind warbled
through the house like a spacious bird,
making it high but lonely.

### Four Small Songs

The sun came out when you were gone.
   I chid him for delay—
he said we had not needed him.
     O prying sun!

What lethargies of loneliness
your letters brought. I read them in
the garret, and the rafters moaned.

The clock purrs and the kitten ticks.
   She catches dandelions,
mistaking them for topaz mice.

   I am going to sleep
   if the rat permit me—
   I hear him singing now
   to the tune of a nut.

## The Deep Stranger

Sometimes as I am drifting
toward my sleep, I dream
I am the deep stranger
smoking his pipe, looking
through his reading glasses,
and sometimes I look out and see
I am not dreaming.

## Brown Study

His son's dinosaurs surround me.
Overhead in his attic study
    antique maps slant away
    between me and the stars.

The kneewall set into the eaves
is sated with books. Down the garret,
    charts and prints cascade from
    the eastern wall—its slit

window—to the western
door with a panel of glass stained
    green and faint lavender,
    the *fleur-de-lis* aqua

in a field of frost. The gable
end displays portraits of him, the boy
    whose ancient animals
    walk this landscape of books,

that pause of space which we call "Father!"

## Nocturne

This is the world that opens and shuts
like the eye of the wax doll
lying in a box
of cast-off things. I hear its breath
in the wind of evening,

in the darkness between planets
and the shining of the stars,
even the whistle
of a boy passing late at night,
or the low of a bird.

## The Amherst Fire

I sprang to the window and each
side of the curtain saw that awful
sun. The moon was shining high and the birds

singing like trumpets, and so much
brighter than day was it that I saw
a caterpillar measure a leaf far

down in the orchard. The innocent
dew was falling and sweet frogs prattling
in the dark pools as if there were no earth.

What, indeed, is Earth but a nest
from whose rim we are all falling?

## A Pearl Jail

This is a stern Winter,
         and in my pearl jail
the cricket and I keep house
      for the frost. No event
of wind or bird breaks the spell

      of steel. I think of sun
            and of Summer as
visages unknown: those were
      the nosegays of twilight
and these—the nosegays of dawn.

      Though it is many nights,
            my mind never comes home.
I find you with dusk, for day
      is tired and lays its
antediluvian cheek

      to the hill like a child.
            Therefore I give you
      good night with fictitious lips,
for to me you have no face.

## May, Merely

The weeds pant
like the center of summer.
I follow my nose
to the dogwood in bloom:

it is May
merely, but Amherst blossoms
in its early heat,
sap oozes from the bark,

and the limbs
are heavy with what may be:
phantom fruit, the seed
in the dusty pollen.

## An Amherst Haiku

Will you bring me a
jacinth for every finger,
and an onyx shoe?

## The Miller's Tale

I am saving a miller moth.
It laid six eggs on the window sill and
I thought it was getting tired,
so I killed it.

Death obtains the rose, but the news
goes no further than the breeze.
The ear is the last face. Today
I slew a mushroom.

### The Naked Eye

The chickens grow very fast—
I am afraid they will be so large
that you cannot perceive them
with the naked eye when you get home.

The flowers have reached the eaves
and are heaving against the roof
which has begun to buckle—
you will have to do something I fear.

We had eggs for breakfast or,
rather, an egg—the yellow yolk
ran under the sideboard, and
it stayed there, refusing to come out.

The cat walking down the stair
makes a great noise—the banister
bulges out as she descends.
The trees in the yard block out the sun—

we are not sure that the sun
still regards us in our small world
with a great eye fully clothed
in the raiment of its rays and beams.

We stumble in the shadows.
The candles speak so slightly that
we can hardly hear their words,
and the moss—the moss is at the door.

## A Morning Picture

A shadow falls upon my
morning picture. The dust falls
on the bureau in your deserted room,

   and gay, frivolous spiders
   spin away in the corners.
I don't go there after dark, for the dayfall

   seems to pause there. I weave for
   the lamp of evening a kind
of twilight before the moon is seen.

## Passing

Autumn is coming on
along the village street.
Chestnut husks lie cloven
    along the walk,
one and another.

The sun is lost. The sky
wears masks of smoke on gray,
and there is moss showing
    upon the oaks,
one and another,
one and another.

The walk is made of slate,
and roots have buckled it.
The child rides, wagoning,
    up and over—
one and another,
one and another,
    how we pass away!

## Theme and Variation

The orchestra of winds performs
its strange, sad music.
I hear it fretting the window-ledge
where the frozen starling sings.

## A New Year

Who is approaching?
Oh, arctic February
    wading through snowdrifts.

I have heard birds sing,
but I fear their bills will be
    frozen closed before

their songs are finished.
Not yet has old King Frost had
    the cold pleasure of

snatching them in his
frigid embrace. Would that we
    might spend this year, now

fleeting swiftly by,
better than the one that we
    cannot now recall.

### Summer's Chariot

Summer is past and gone;
Autumn with the sere and yellow leaf
is already upon us.

Someone must have oiled
his chariot wheels, for I did not
hear him pass. And what report

has he borne to heaven
of misspent time and wasted hours?
Each moment in its season—

now we wear our golden
tresses done up in net-caps.

## Small Victory

At noon I heard a well-known rap.
A friend I love *so* dearly came
and asked me to ride in the woods,
 the sweet, still woods.

I said I could not go; he said
he wanted me very much. Oh,
I struggled with great temptation.
 It cost me much

of denial, but in the end
I conquered—not a glorious
triumph, where you hear the rolling
 drum, but a kind

of helpless victory which comes
of itself, not faintest music,
weary soldiers, nor a waving
 flag, nor a long,

loud shout, only a small silence,
a pause, a stillness at the heart.

## Housekeeping

The sun has barely
risen, and I am in
mourning, for the house is being
cleaned—I prefer pestilence: that

is more classic and
less fell. I wear my cap
awry to frighten the spiders
a-dangle in the corners.

I have been at work
scaring the timorous dust,
being obedient and kind.
I am the Queen of the Court,

if regalia be
dust and dirt. I have three
loyal subjects; like a martyr,
I serve and sweep before them

in bonds of despair.
I survey my kitchen
and pray for kind deliverance.
*My* kitchen, I called it! God

keep me in His Majesty
from what they call *households*!

## Among the Stones

Tonight it is cool and quiet,
the toil of the feverish day forgotten.
Some of my friends are gone,
and some of my friends are sleeping—
sleeping the churchyard sleep.

I have walked there sweet summer
evenings and read the names on the stones, wondered
who would come and give me
the like memorial. There will be
no sun or singing birds

in the coming spring. I shall
look for an early June then, when the grass is
growing green; I shall love
to call the bird there if it has
a gentle music; the

meekest-eyed wildflowers,
and the low, plaintive insect. How *precious* is
the grave when aught we love
is laid there, and affection would
go too, if the lost were lonely.

## First Snow

A thousand little winds wafted
to me this morning an air
fragrant with forest leaves and bright

autumnal berries. Now and then
a gray leaf fell. Crickets sang
all day long. High in a crimson

tree a belated bird trembled—
there must be many moments
in an eternal day. Alas!

I remember the leaves were falling,
and now there are falling snows.
Are not leaves the brethren of snows?

I dream of being a grandam
and binding my silver hairs,
the children dancing around me.

## Delay

I have tried to delay the frosts,
I have coaxed the fading flowers,
I thought I would detain a few
    of the crimson leaves,

but their companions call them—they
cannot stay away. You will find
blue hills with autumnal shadows
    silently sleeping

on them: there will be a glory
lingering round the day. You will know
autumn has come and gone his way
    through the acorn wood

wrapping his faded cloak about him.

## Company

How I love to see them, a beautiful company
coming down the hill crusted with snow,
wearing its blue mantilla,
which men call the future. Their hearts are
full of joy, and their hands of gladness.

The bouquet was not withered, nor was the bottle cracked
when they arrived singing, but the wind
whispered so violently,
and it grew so cold, that we gathered
all the quinces in, put up the stove

in the sitting-room, and bade the world good-by. These brief,
imperfect meetings have their own tales
to tell—we shall hear them
when the nails hang full of coats again,
and the chairs hang full of hats, and I

can count the slippers under the kitchen chair.

## An Amherst Pastoral

Today is very beautiful—
just as bright, just as blue, just as green
    and as white and as crimson

as the cherry trees full in bloom,
and the half-opening peach blossoms,
    and the grass just as waving,

and the sky and hill and cloud can
make it, if they try. When the west
    wind blows, the pines lift their light

leaves and make sweet music. You will
awaken in dust, in the ceaseless
    din of the untiring

city. Wouldn't you change your dwelling
    for my palace in the dew?

# Death

There is a subject on which
we never touch. Ignorance
of its pageantries does not deter me.
I too went out to meet the dust

early in the morning. I
too in daisy mounds possess
hid treasure. I write you from the summer,
and frogs sincerer than our own

splash in their Maker's pools. Oh,
dew upon the bloom fall yet again
upon a summer's night! Of such have been
the frauds which have vanquished faces,

sown plant of flesh the church-yard
plats, and occasioned angels.
When you hear the new violet sucking
her way among the sods, shall you

be resolute? Many can
boast a hollyhock, but few
can bear a rose. Distinctly sweet your face
stands in its phantom niche. How brief,

from vineyards and the sun—for
in the merriest flower there is
a pensive air, but fairer colors than
mine are twined while stars are shining.

## Asea

I am pleasantly located
in the deep sea. The shore is safer,
   but I love to buffet Ocean—

I can count the little wrecks here
in these still depths, hear the murmuring winds.
   Oh! I love the danger! Love will row

   you out, if her hands are strong. Don't wait
until I land where you stand peering
   into the humming gale, for I

am going ashore on the other side.

## Just God

Who writes these funny accidents
    where railroads meet each other
quite unexpectedly, and gentlemen
    in factories get their heads cut off
    quite informally? The Author

    relates them in such a sprightly
        way, they are quite attractive.
If prayers had any answers to them,
    I should not know the question, for I
        seek and I don't find and knock and

    it is not opened. I wonder
        if God is just—presume that
He is, and 'twas only a blunder of
    Matthew's. Heaven is large, isn't it?
        Then when one is done, is there not

    another, and—then—if God
    is willing, we are neighbors then.

## A Dream of Roses

I thought I would write again.
  I write many letters
  with pens which are not seen—

do you receive them? I think
  of you today, and dreamed
  of you all last night. When

father rapped upon my door
  to wake me this morning,
  I was walking with you

in a wonderful garden,
  and helping you to pick—
  roses, and although we

gathered them with all our might,
  the basket was never
  full. Therefore, all day I

pray that I may walk with you,
  gather roses again,
  and as the night draws on,

it pleases me, and I count
  impatiently the hours
  between me and darkness,

the dream of you and roses,
  and the basket never full.

## Lamps

I love to have the lamps shine
on the evening table,
but I am out with lanterns
looking for myself—and now
this falling snow sternly and silently

lifts up its hand between. While
I sit among the snows, that
summer day—on which the bees
came and the south wind—turns to
phantoms and vanishes slow away. How

many years, I wonder, will
sow the moss upon them till
we bind again? As many
as the suns that shine between
our lives and loss, and violets—not last

year's, but having the mother's
eyes. Is wish not the world turned
dream? I often wish that I
were grass, whom all these problems
of the dust might not terrify. What is

this carnal chill, zero at
the bone, but a book of leaves?
Sometimes I wonder, nodding,
if I ever dreamed, then if
I am dreaming now, then if I always

dreamed, and there is not a world.

## Fading Things

If roses had not faded,
  and frosts had never come,
and one had not fallen here
and there whom I could not waken,

there were no need of Heaven
  other than this below.
I love these fading things—where
they go when summer's done, only

the thyme knows, and the robin
  who, when the west winds come,
winks and away forever
till the next eternity.

## An Orator of Feather

*Summer?* Was there a summer?
I saw the fields go—dancer and floor
    and cadence gathered away,
and I—a phantom—rehearse the story!
    An orator of feather unto

an audience of fuzz. I
found a bird this morning—down—down—on
    a little bush at the foot
of the garden. "And wherefore sing," I said,
    "since nobody hears?" But he replied,

"My business it is to sing,
for the supper of the heart is when
    the guest is gone. Pardon
my sanity in a world insane." He
    puffed his feathers out and lofted song,

but he left me with a quill.

## The Winter Garden

It is November. The noons are more
laconic and the sundowns sterner.
   November always seemed to me
the Norway of the year. A neighbor

put her child into an ice nest last
Monday forenoon. Sharper than dying
   is the death for the dying's sake.
I cannot stoop to strut in a world

where bells toll—frost is no respecter
of persons, and yet the wind blows gay
   today; jays bark like blue terriers.
My heart is red as February

and purple as March, for I taste life—
it is a vast morsel. If we knew
   how deep the crocus lay, we should
never let her go. The gentian is

a greedy flower, and overtakes
us all. Although death grasps the proudest
   zinnia from my purple garden,
blossoms belong to the bee. I would

eat evanescence slowly—my Winter
flowers are near and foreign. I have
   only to cross the floor to stand
among the Isles of Spice and Summer.

## Adventure

A circus passed the house this morning—
I followed it along the street
beneath the summer oaks, among the folk

staring at Africa on parade.
When I came to myself and saw
how far I had come away, how many

of us were strangers, I turned and ran.
I have just shot past the corner,
now the wayside houses, and the gate flies

open to see me coming home. Still
I feel the red in my mind—though
the drums are out—the echo of the flags.

## Winter Bouquet

It storms in Amherst five days—
it snows, and then it rains, and then
soft fogs like veils hang on all the houses,
and then the days turn topaz

like a lady's pin. The hills
take off their purple frocks and dress
in long white nightgowns. The men were
mowing the second hay not

long since—the cocks were smaller
than the first, and spicier. I
would distill a cup, bear it to my friends,
drinking to summer no more

astir, make a balloon of
a dandelion, but the fields
are gone where children walked the tangled road,
some of them to the end, some

but a little way, even
as far as the fork. Remembrance
is more sweet than robins in May orchards.
Today is very cold, yet

I have much bouquet upon
the window pane—of moss and fern.
I call them saints' flowers, because they do
not romp as other flowers

do, but stand so still and white.
I enjoy much with a precious
fly, not one of your blue monsters, but a
timid creature that hops from

pane to pane of her white house
so very cheerfully, and hums
and thrums—a sort of speck piano. I
have one new bird and several

trees of old ones. A snow slide
from the roof dispelled the sweetbrier.
There are as yet no streets, though the sun is
riper. This is a landscape

of frost and zeros. I wish
"the faith of the fathers" didn't
wear brogans and carry blue umbrellas.
The doubt, like the mosquito,

buzzes round my faith. My heart
has flown before, my breaking voice
follows—that bareheaded life under grass
worries me like a wasp—life

of flowers lain in flowers—
what a home of dew to come to!
We reckon by the fruit. When the grape gets
by, and the pippin and the

chestnut—when the days are a
little short by the clock, and a
little long by the lack—when the sky has
new red gowns and a purple

bonnet, I am glad that kind
of time goes by. Twilight is but
the short bridge, and the moon stands at the end.
With Nature in my ruche, I

shall not miss the spring, the seasons falling
and the leaves—the moulting goldfinch singing.

## Flowers in Season

### i. Spring

Such a purple morning, even to
the morning-glory that climbs the cherry tree.
Crocuses came up, in the garden
off the dining room, and a fuchsia
like willowy strawberries—

primroses, and heliotrope by
the aprons full—the mountain-colored one—and
a jessamine bud with an odor
like lupine—gillyflowers, magenta,
a few mignonette, and sweet

alyssum bountiful—carnation
buds. The ice-house is filled to make tumblers cool
next summer, and now and then a cream.
I spent some moments profitably
with the South Sea rose. I have

removed a geranium leaf or
two, supplied a lily in the parlor vase.
The sweet-peas are unchanged, and the fields
give brawny promise of haycocks by
and by.

### ii. Fall

North Wind has arrived—
the trees stand right up straight when they hear
his boots, and will bear crockery wares
instead of fruit, I fear. He hasn't
starched the geraniums yet, but will
have ample time. I pick up

tufts of mignonette, and the sweet
alyssum for winter—these red and
   gold and ribbon days seem as dim as
   Winter. Faded petals proffer me
      colors from the vault of Earth—

nothing has happened but loneliness,
perhaps too daily to relate. With love for
   supper—if deferred it will fade like
   ice cream—the moon is morning's memoir.
      Take the key to the lily

   now, and I will lock the rose.

## Late Summer

In the dooryard a stand of milkweed
  draws the gorging honeybees,
  and in the oak a squirrel
treads, nattering of the impending

fall. The skies are blue and yellow, and
  there's a purple craft or so
  in which a friend could sail. I
feel as the band does before it makes

its first shout—a catbird clothed in gray
  patrols the goldenrod, drops
  over the sod bank toward
the road—he stops now and then to cry

his ownership. Pray, what does he keep
  of the sweet season beyond
  the shape of the maple leaf,
and the swift, waning sun? I could play

  in the woods till dark—till you
  take me where sundowns cannot find us.

## Late Fall

The stove is singing the merry song
of the wood—it is sweet and antique
as birds—not a flake assaults
them but it freezes me. Though

the sailor cannot see the north, he
knows the needle can. I dreamed last night
I heard bees fight for pond-
lily stamens, and I waked

with a fly in my room making grim
ado of death—'twas much of a mob
as I could master. This is
a mighty morning. Too few

the mornings be, too scant the nights—how
long the days that make the flesh afraid.

## Amherst Neighbors

Do you recall old Mrs. Ay,
    with the nose of a hawk?
    Last Monday-week she fledged
her antique wings and soared
    to her nest in Heaven.

Bee and Cee are closest comrades
    still. Together they walk,
    talk, eat—vote together!
They intend to be Jonathan
    and David, or Damon

and Pythias, or what's better,
    the United States of
    America! Mrs.
Dee grows larger, rolls down the lane
    to church like a marble.

I found Miss Ea in our garden
    peering at a purloined lily—
    bats think foxes have no
eyes. It comforts the criminal
    little to know the law

expires with him. Father feels ill—
    the straightest engine has
    its leaning hour. Madame
Gee goes tattling still. Her yard needs
    combing—no one can keep

a sumach and a secret too.
　　And there is Aitch, of course—
　　she looks a little tart,
but makes excellent pies after
　　one gets acquainted. I

tend house and to a quiet hour,
　　Miss Jaye grows so thin
　　in her cottage of slats,
I could fancy that skeleton
　　cats caught spectre

rats in dim old nooks and corners.
　　Mr. Kaye is less lively
　　than he was wont, if one might
discern it—there are those in the
　　morgue that bewitch us with

sweetness, but that which is dead must
　　go with the ground. To speak
　　of wings yet again—sweet
Mrs. Elle comes with the robins.
　　Robins have wings. Mrs.

Elle has wings. A society
for the prevention of wings would
be of benefit to us all.

## Passages

### i.

The crocuses are with us
and several other colored friends.
There is a tree in the woods
that shivers. I am afraid it is
cold. I am going to make it a little

coat. I must make several,
because it is tall as the barn, and
put them on as the circus
men stand on each other's shoulders. I
hear robins a great way off, and wagons a

great way off, and rivers a
great way off, and all appear to be
hurrying somewhere undisclosed
to me. Even the wren upon her nest
knows more than daisy dares—we must be careful

what we say. No bird resumes
its egg.

### ii.

The colors quiver upon
the pastures and day goes gay
to the northwest. Oh that beloved
witch-hazel! It looks like tinsel fringe combined

with staider fringes, witch and
witching too. It haunts me like childhood's
Indian pipe, or ecstatic
puff-balls, or that mysterious apple
that sometimes comes on river-pinks—and a dim

suggestion of dandelion,
if her hair were raveled and she grew
   upon a twig rather than
a tube.

iii.

What an exchange of awe! I
suppose the wild flowers encourage themselves
   by the dim woods. Two or three
finches in plush teams reined nearer to
   the window, but the bird that
is bruised limps to his house in silence.
We will miss the nasturtiums, but we will meet

   the chestnuts.

iv.

I open my
window and it fills my chamber with
   white dirt. I think God must be
dusting. Slips of the last rose repose
in kindred soil with waning bees. How softly

summer shuts without the creaking of a door.

## Epistle

Evening called with a twilight of you.
The men were picking up the apples today,
 and the pretty boarders left the trees,
birds and ants and bees. I heard the chipper say
 "Dee" six times in disapprobation.

His bombazine reproof falls still on
the twilight, and checks the softer uproars of
 departing day, for how should *we* like
to have our privileges wheeled away in
 a barrel? We had two hurricanes

within as many hours, one of which
came near enough to untie my apron—but
 this moment the hens are warbling.
A man of anonymous wits is making
 a garden in the lane to set out

slips of bluebird—the moon grows from the seed. I
 send you a robin who is eating
a remnant oat upon the sill of the barn.

## An Amherst Christmas

Atmospherically, it was the most
       beautiful Christmas. The hens
   came to the door with Santa Claus,
the pussies washed themselves in the air
without chilling their tongues. Visitors

from the chimney were a new dismay,
       and the friends at the barn were
   so happy! Maggie gave the hens
a check for potatoes, each cat  had
a gilt-edged bone, and the horse had new

blankets from Boston. Will the sweet child
       who sent me the butterflies,
   herself a member of the same
ethereal nation, accept a
rustic kiss flavored, we trust, with clover?

## Poetry

Memory's fog is rising: I had a terror
   I could tell to none—and so I sing,
   as the boy does in the burying-ground,
because I am afraid. When a sudden light
on the orchards, or a new fashion in the wind

troubled my attention, I felt a palsy,
   here, the verses just relieve.
                    I am
small, like the wren, and my hair is bold,
like the chestnut burr, and my eyes like sherry
in the glass the guest leaves. There is always one

thing to be grateful for—that one is one's self
   and not somebody else. "We thank thee,
   oh loving Father," for these strange minds
that enamor us against Thee.
                  If I read
a book, and it makes my body so cold no

fire can ever warm me, I know *that* is
   poetry. If I feel physically
   as if the top of my head were
taken off, I know *that* is poetry. These are
the only ways I know it. Is there any

other way?
          How does the poet learn to grow,
   or is it unconveyed, like witchcraft
   or melody? I had no monarch
in my life and cannot rule myself. When I
try to organize, my little force explodes,

leaves me bare and charred. I marked a line in one
     verse, because I met it after I
     made it and never consciously touch
a paint mixed by another person. I do
not let go of it, because it is mine.

Two editors of journals came and asked me
     for my mind. When I asked them, "Why?" they
     said I was penurious—they'd use it
for the world. I could not weigh my self myself—
my size felt small to me. One hears of Mister

Whitman—I never read his book, but was told
     he is disgraceful. To my thought, "To
     publish" is foreign as firmament
to fin. My barefoot rank is better. If fame
belonged to me, I could not escape her—if

she did not, the longest day would pass me on
     the chase.
               There seems a spectral power
     in thought that walks alone. I find
ecstasy in living—the mere sense of life
is joy enough. The chestnut hit my notice

suddenly, and I thought the skies in blossom!

## An Amherst Calendar

### January

The vane defies the wind.

### February

                              It is warm now.
A mellow rain is falling.
It won't be ripe till April. How luscious
is the dripping of February eaves!
            It makes our thinking pink.

It antedates the robin.

### March

                        Who would be
ill a-bed in March, that month
of proclamations? Sleigh-bells and blue-jays
contend in my matinee, and the North
            surrenders instead of

the South—a reverse of bugles.

### April

                              And now
    arbutus is knitting pink
clothes.

### May

        The apple-blossoms yesterday were
slightly disheartened by a snow-storm, but
            the birds encouraged them

all that they could, and how fortunate that
   the little ones had come to
cheer their damask brethren! We have inland
buttercups, as out-of-door flowers are
      still at sea. The seed sown

in the lake bears the liquid flower.

### June

                              There is
   a circus here, and Farmers'
Commencement, boys and girls from Tripoli,
and Governors and swords parade the streets.
      They lean upon the fence

that guards the quiet churchyard ground, and jar
   the grass, now warm and soft as
a tropic nest.

### July

            Sweet-peas stand in carmine
sheaves. The fuchsia is a bliss of sorrow.

### August

      In the garden scarlet

carnations with a witching suggestion,
   and hyacinths covered with
promises, nod and beckon, beckon and
nod.

### September

The red leaves take the green leaves' place, and
the landscape yields. We go

to sleep with the peach and wake with the stone,
yet the stone is the pledge of
summers to come.

### October

My garden vanished with
beautiful reluctance, like an evening star.
There are sticks of rowan

for the stove—chopped by bees—and butterflies
stacked the cords on Saturday
afternoons. I am kept busy picking
up stems and stamens, as the hollyhocks
have left their clothes around.

### November

I had the luxury of a mother
until November. She slipped
from our fingers like a flake gathered by
the wind. The anguish was also granted
me to see the first snow

fall next day upon her grave.

### December

I have no
letter from the dead, yet daily love them
more. Instead, a jay drops me a note—
blue on white. He asks me to begin again,
that bleeding beginning every mourner knows.

## The Clock

### i.

The geese make a sound like vee in the air
as they pass homing to the South.
'Tis not long since the fields
could not remember frost.

I grope through drifts of awe as I settle
into Autumn, reflecting that
the grapes were big and fresh,
tasting like emerald dew.

The Summer's picture is not yet mottled
by the snow. My window frames it—
the orchard recalling
its dream of sweet burden

against a sky that is falling to Earth.
Time seeps from the clock behind me—
I hear it splash like glass
melting in mists of breath.

### ii.

Except for the tapping of the clock,
it is quiet in the room. The floor
has a paisley skin on oaken
bones. Along the walls, books
walk the shelves, stop

at casements where a wan sun falls in
on pools of shadow. I am sitting
in an arm-chair considering
this flow of moments, drift
of hours. Each rap

of the pendulum laboring here,
in this quarry of silence, transmutes
    itself, becomes its own echo,
        a retracing between
            wood and crystal

of what comes to pass. The quarry fills
with emptiness seeping through the chinks
    of sound, between tick and tick—there
        are droplets falling from
            the tap of time.

*iii.*

I study the clock, regard
its face—it is my own, my hands
    that swing their arcs through numerals
        that mark me at my meals,
the funerals of friends, the pillow sighs
        that summon sleep from dream,

    that take me down to verges
    beyond which I may just discern
    the figures of the lost, the shades
        that bide and wake. It is
the face of the familiar and the strange—
        my image lurks upon

    the glass, sinks through, and travels
    with the moon of brass in its pace
    and shining pause, the falling and
            ascension—eyes and mouth,
lips, brow and cheeks caught swinging in the bright
        machinery of time.

*iv.*

It is as near as though
I can see it—the river
    of time flowing out
      of the clock—

a clear stream, like air, but
more crystalline. It is as
    though a cataract
      made of sun

and shadow spills into
the room among the tables
    and chairs, begins to
      wash against

the claws of the divan,
the leg of the candlestand—
    begins to deepen
      over the dim

design of the carpet.
It is a tide rising to
    fathom the corners
      of my space.

*v.*

There are voices in the flow
of time cascading down the wall,
    out of the clock. It is hard
      for me to discern shapes
caught in the quick crystal river

deepening about my feet,
lifting to my ankles, my knees.
But as the fluid air moves
        to the level of my breast,
as the river slows and deepens,

        becoming instead a tarn,
I make out the little figures
        at last—floating and drowning,
                flailing and calling out.
They are naked. Their eyes are bright,

        their skins glisten. I feel the suck
of the undertow on my flesh.
        In the center of the room
                a vortex is forming—
they are all being drawn into

        the whirlpool—it is taking
them down, these people caught in time.
        They grasp at my shoulders, now
                awash, attempt to claw
ashore—I must try to save them!

vi.

I lift my hands out of time. I stand.
I stare hard at the clear ocean stream.
*Stop!* I cry, and *Stop!* again—all stops.
        Time freezes in its wash.

Like insects caught in amber, the folk
lie jeweled in their eddies. Shadow
and lamplight deckle them. Sunset glows
        in the dark window-pane.

The ice of time engulfs golden oak,
mahogany and teak, warp and weft
of fabric—drape, couch, and carpet. On
   the wall the paper scrolls.

In its cradle the globe floats. The hands
of the clock mark the Apocalypse—
it is of no moment at long last.
   The vortex vanishes.

No chime begins its song, no stroke ends.
The chain is weightless. Eternity
is now and only now. Let it go—
   go with it—let them go.

vii.

I wind the clock and time begins
to wind. Life begins to windle.
The room becomes the room in which I dwell.
   All is as it was and cannot

be again—no part of mind is
permanent. Though this may startle
the happy, it assists the sad. I will
   make do, then—I will make time do

those things it would have done at any rate.

# Essays by Various Hands

Knock with
tremor.
These are Caesars.
Should they be at Home
Flee as if you
trod unthinking
On the foot of Doom —

                receded   to   accosted

These      succeeded
                        summons.
from      your   summits   subjects
Centuries ago.    subjects
Should they       substance
rend you    with "How
are you"
What have    you to show?

JEANNE HOLLAND

# "Knock with / tremor":
# When Daughters Revise "Dear Father"

Sometime near 1874, on a small worksheet, Emily Dickinson wrote the following poem:

> Knock with tremor—
> These are Caesars—
> Should they be at Home
> Flee as if you trod unthinking
> On the Foot of Doom—
>
> These seceded from your summons
> Centuries ago—
> Should they rend you with "How are you"
> What have you to show?

On the other side of the sheet, Dickinson wrote:

> Dear Father—

> Emily

Commenting on this cryptic, unfinished letter, Thomas Johnson states, "Her father died 16 June 1874. One conjectures that the unwritten message expresses the void she felt his passing had created."[1]

However, I would like to examine how the biographical

reference of this void might translate into a larger rhetorical significance.[2] "Knock with / tremor," Dickinson's cautionary poem about summoning Caesars, and her empty letter to her father profoundly emblematize a woman writer's negotiation of patriarchal authority. But in the gaps and silences of this document, in the space that stretches between father and daughter, we also find the effaced presence of the mother. The daughter's revision of the oedipal drama, I will argue, illuminates the gendered stakes of representation: the problematics of feminine subjectivity, the limitations of logos (or the Father's Law), and the erasure of the mother's body.[3]

In order to appreciate more fully how this text inscribes paternal law and maternal semiotics, it should be examined in manuscript form:

> Knock with
> tremor—
> These are Caesars—
> Should they be at Home
> Flee as if you
> trod unthinking
> On the Foot of Doom—
>
> These   <sub>receded to—accostal</sub>
>   seceded
> from your summons
>     summits
>     subjects
>     substance
> Centuries ago—
> Should they
> rend you with "How
> are you"
> What have you to show?

In line 9, Dickinson lists three choices for the word which eventually became "summons." Dissatisfied with "summits," "subjects," and "substance," Dickinson wrote above them, "receded to—*accostal*," as a possible phrase to be appended to "These." Then something made her think of the word "summons." She slashed through the previous substitutions, writing "summons" once above "summits" and again up the right side of the margin. In manuscript, the final question "What have you to show?" is urgent. Dickinson underlined the question, albeit in her typical manner, irregularly and sporadically. Four dashes are drawn between and beneath five words. Perhaps Johnson ignores the underlining because it's not possible to tell which particular words should be emphasized. At any rate, "What have you to show?" is not italicized in the Johnson edition.

Instead of reading the Johnson version, with its regularized hymnal meter and quatrains, I propose that we examine "Knock with / tremor" in manuscript: its spasmodic gait, I will argue, more clearly reveals Dickinson's challenge to patrilinearity and power. The manuscript strategically stumbles, fracturing linearity as it reproduces the transgression it warns against. The poem begins by addressing an erased "you." Cast in the imperative voice, the poem addresses "you" as both subject and object; "you" is a figure located in the conventionally feminine position as suppliant to a powerful male figure. To warn "you" that pursuing "Caesars" is a perilous undertaking, the imperative "Knock with" is truncated as "tremor" is isolated on line 2. This broken warning/command conveys both fearfulness—the one who knows better can barely speak—and determination—she emphasizes "tremor" to caution her reader. Significantly, the poem first reproduces a regularized meter, a relict of androcentric literary genres, in line 3, which identifies the Caesars. The longest line yet in the poem, "Should they be at Home," places "Home" at its end/destination, although whether the home is occupied or empty cannot be determined due to the "Should" which begins the line/journey.

In the first stanza, it is not even known if these imperious, powerful male figures are at Home. But *should* they be, the feminized "you" is warned to "Flee." Her open pursuit is a breach of decorum, an improper act—comparable to stepping clumsily on someone's foot.[4] This particular transgression, however, is much more enormous; it is as if the heedless seeker trod upon the foot of "Doom." When in line 5 the poem first explicitly focuses on the supplicant, "Flee as if you" makes an incomplete line. Again the effaced feminine "you" is addressed. If these powerful fathers are home, "you" should flee. The incomplete line momentarily raises the question of responsibility, as if I did what? As the poem unfolds, this riddle will prove insoluable.

In line 6, "trod unthinking" occupies the entire line as if to convey the enormity of the supplicant's naivete. Although it begins the next line, "trod" is uncapitalized, suggesting the woman's unconsciousness of the act. At any moment, she might carelessly misstep. And a slip-up will bring retribution.

With the regular "On the Foot of Doom—", the father's presence makes itself curiously felt in line 7. When the father's foot is spoken of, the line is trochaic; its heavy/soft beat marks an advance/retreat movement reflecting the father's presence/absence. That the father's "Foot" is described as the Foot of "Doom" insinuates the deadliness of patriarchal literary forms, such as regularized meters and prescribed genres, for women writers. This notion is further reinforced by the echo between this line and the previous "Should they be at Home." Home is Doom: forms of familiar containment prove at once comforting and deadly for a woman writer. The reader learns that she cannot walk in the father's shoes; she can only step on his feet in a kind of "unthinking" gait.

As if she fears she will not be heeded, the speaker intensifies her exhortations in the second stanza. Because the Caesars "seceded"—violently broke away—from the supplicant's summons, her imperative call, "Centuries ago—", their retreat is absolute and always already has been. Pursuit is futile.

The second stanza knots up as it attempts to figure the father's absence. Dickinson's first choice for line 8, "These seceded" appropriates the post-Civil War awareness of the violence in the word "secession." This unlawful absenting which divided a house against itself recalls the father-daughter separation and the pain associated with that rending. Because she was displeased with her choices for the next line ("from your summits/subjects/substance"), however, Dickinson substituted "receded *to—accostal*" above line 8. A violation of the expected idiom "receded from," "receded *to accostal*" depicts the speaker's confusion as to the location of the Caesars and her responsibility for their departure. In this line, their "receding from" her accostal is muted; the male authorities have receded "to" an accostal. The specular structure of this neologism reflects both that the male authorities receded in response "to" her accostal and that she perceives their retreat as an accostal "to" her. That "*to—accostal*" is underlined only highlights its controversion of linear reasoning.

What rescues "These seceded" is Dickinson's subsequent discovery of "summons." Dickinson's reiteration of "summons" and her revision of the poem based upon it authorizes some biographical speculation on our part. According to Blackstone, whose *Commentaries on the Laws of England* Edward Dickinson studied as a law student, a summons is "a warning to appear in court at the return of the original writ, given to the defendant by two of the sheriff's messengers called summoners, either in person or left at his house or land. . . ."[5] With this legalistic term, the poet decides to maintain the "seceded / *from*" [my emphasis] relationship. Implicating Dickinson's own lawyer father in the breach, "summons" asks, what right had he to depart?[6]

As if these warnings are not sufficient, the poem takes another step in cautioning the reader. Conditionally, the poem fulfills the suppliant's fantasy, granting her recognition from the imperious male figures ("Should they / rend you with "How / are you"). Yet the dream of paternal presence proves the ultimate horror. Should the Caesars acknowledge the seeker, speak to her in even the most mundane of greetings, "How are you," she would be dismembered, as if her "you," her identity, was predicated on a paternal neglect, or a Father's

No. Initially the poem's final question seems as rhetorical and innocent as the greeting the poet imagines the Caesars would proffer. "What have you to show?" may be interpreted conventionally as, What will you have gained for your troubles? The implied answer is, Not much. But this rhetorical question may also be taken literally.[7] After the seeker is torn apart by the Caesars' recognition of her, what will she have to show *then*? What sort of figure would she present?

We see the effects of that departure in the concluding lines. Unlike "Should they be at home" in the first stanza, the final conditional inquiry, occurring in the shadow of the futile summons, is fragmented: "Should they / rend you with 'How / are you.'" These rended lines figure the breakdown of the law and the fragmentation of the daughter which the poem rehearses. The colloquial "How are you" becomes notable, becomes an outlaw, by the poem's splitting it across two lines. For how may one be rended by "how"? How questions in what manner, in what way one accomplishes a task. And that is what this poem is all about: how. How does a daughter approach a father? On what grounds and in what way does she proceed? The urgency of this how is contained within the unremarkable "How" of "How are you. " The language we use every day, therefore, reveals/conceals the daughter's struggle for legitimation.

"What have you  to  show?" the poet queries the daughter who would be satisfied. The relation of the jagged line drawn erratically underneath and the question it underscores indicate the outcome of pursuing Caesars. As with "How are you, " it would initially appear that a mundane language has intruded into the poem. Rather the poem's knowledge of the much-noted absent father and the silenced, effaced mother *extrude* into our nonreflective "use" of language in the conventional query, What have you to show? The jagged line beneath the familiar question confronts the daughter at once with the urgency of making sense, of stringing together the line and answering the query, and of her own awareness of the fictionality of such wholeness. In the end, what she will have to show is precisely figured as a question and a broken line.

At this point, we should turn to the other face of the document, Dickinson's empty letter to her father. What is the relation between the poem and this cryptogram? The letter's central empty space which has usurped narrative, I will argue, figures the erased mother; this silence suggests the repression of the maternal body demanded by the ascension of the symbolic.

A feminine, silent "nothing" which connects/intercedes between father and daughter—this description of the hollow inside of Dickinson's letter echoes biographers' descriptions of her mother, Emily Norcross Dickinson. When we search for information regarding the poet's mother, we are struck by the repeated assertions of her *nothingness*. One of Dickinson's first biographers, George Frisbie Whicher describes Emily Norcross as "the type of gentle, submissive woman that stirs the possessive and protective instincts of intensely masculine men.... She reverenced her husband and devoted her life to making his home a silken nest. Both were content that he should be the integer and she the cipher that 'swelled the man's amount.'"[8] Richard Chase concurs: "About her there seems to have been almost nothing to say.... She figures hardly at all in the meager store of what we know about the Dickinson family, and one gathers from this that she was unusually passive and retiring and possessed no ostensible power of being or mind."[9] Of course, Dickinson herself encourages such dismissal by characterizing her mother as one who "does not care for thought" (letter 261). In perhaps the most famous reference, the poet told Higginson, "I never had a mother" (letter 342b).

Early on, Barbara Clarke Mossberg helped illuminate this shadowy maternal figure and her talented daughter's vexed relation to her. More recently, Cynthia Griffin Wolff's interpretation of the courtship of Emily Norcross and Edward Dickinson has revolutionized our understanding of the mother's reticence and the home from which her daughter later emerged. Wolff reads the letters Edward and Emily exchanged from 1826 to 1828, while he was a twenty-three-year-old lawyer beginning his practice in Amherst and she a twenty-two-year-old woman living on her father's farm several miles away in Monson. Compared to courtship letters exchanged by other couples in early nineteenth-century America, what emerges with shocking clarity is Edward's voluble narcissism and Emily's passive-aggressiveness. From reading Edward's bombastic letters, Wolff points out, we learn what qualities he valued in a model wife, but nothing in particular about Emily Norcross.[10] When we read the letters of Emily Norcross, however, the mystery deepens. As Wolff observes, "The most striking fact is that she wrote so little—twenty-three notes in all, scarcely any of them covering more than one side of a letter sheet. If Edward was long-winded and impersonal, Emily was all but mute" (38). Wolff's analysis bears quoting in detail:

> [V]ery early in the dance of courtship, one characteristic of Emily Norcross's mode of communication emerged with startling clarity: she preferred never to speak for herself. It was not that she was pliant or unselfish or without personal wishes (although Edward imputed all of these traits to her in his more optimistic moments); she communicated her wishes indirectly, through a complex and often inefficient game of verbal hide-and-seek. Instead of laboring to speak out, she withheld communication entirely; confronted with her unchanging inarticulateness, Edward was forced to guess at her preferences. Ironically, his habit of bossy volubility was an asset to her here, for she could consistently count on him to elaborate a plan for her to follow or to "presume" what her silence might mean; he would go on with this guessing (becoming increasingly impatient) until at last he hit upon the correct formulation. Then, and only then, she would respond. (39)

The intensity of Emily's withholding was most dramatically illuminated when Edward wrote to propose marriage: she did not respond until two months later. This was four months since she had previously written. By analyzing the husband's self-centered ambitions, obtuseness, and bewilderment, and the wife's increasing withdrawal, Wolff follows the early pattern of mis- and incommunication, substantiating that the Dickinson marriage was not a happy one.

The Dickinson home was characterized by the ultimate failure of the father's language and the power of the mother's silences. The cipher or nothing that "Mother" signified reverberates throughout Dickinson's poetry. Wolff writes: "'Mother' exists most directly and vividly in her daughter's style of communication, her use of language, and her attitude toward words—their power and their limitation. . . . No other American poet has understood so well the power of *withholding* communication, of remaining quiet in lieu of speaking—of being parsimonious with language and using ellipses rather than proliferations of words" (52).

But as daughter-poet, Dickinson is caught in-between her parents and the symbolic and semiotic modes of discourse: as a writer, she must speak the father's symbolic discourse which perpetuates the subjection, silencing, of the mother. But as a poet, by framing the emptiness and calling attention to the silence, she illuminates what has been repressed. She does not fill in the gaps; unlike her father in the courtship letters, she does not speak for the mother. Instead she maintains the indecipherability of the mother's desire, radically undermining any totalization of paternal authority.

The empty letter, I would argue, identifies the absent/present feminine "you" which is so problematically addressed on the other side. The absent "you" addressed in the imperatives suggests the mother's body which is utterly erased in the center of the letter. Since representation is predicated on the loss of the mother's body, that body cannot be re-produced. What we have instead is a sign, a feminized "you," which appears at points in "Knock with / tremor." In the letter, however, the poet herself occupies the space of that "you"; *she* approaches the Caesar by addressing "Dear Father." But the blank maternal space protects her from being rent; this silence is what she wanted to tell him, this "Pause of Space" is what she has to show. At the bottom of the letter, she signs "Emily," which is also her mother's name.

At the end of *No Man's Land*, Gilbert and Gubar ask: "Isn't it . . . possible that the primordial self/other couple from whom we learning the couplings, doublings, and splitting of 'hierarchy' is the couple called 'mother/child' rather than the one called 'man/woman'? If this is so, isn't it also possible that verbal signification arises not from a confrontation with the 'Law of the Father' but from a consciousness of the lure and the lore of the mother?"[11] Rather than privileging *either* paternal law or maternal semiotic, Dickinson merely proceeds, in her spasmodic gait, to dance upon her toes.

## Notes

1. These comments and the version of poem 1325 which I have reproduced are taken from what is considered to be the standard edition of Emily Dickinson's poetry, *The Complete Poems of Emily Dickinson*, ed. Thomas H. Johnson, 3 vols. (Cambridge, MA: Harvard University Press, 1963) 3: 916 17. I argue, however, for an alternate edition of Dickinson's poetry, one which respects the particularities and eccentricities of her poetic line breaks. Whenever possible, readers should consult Dickinson's poems in *The Manuscript Books of Emily Dickinson*, ed. Ralph W. Franklin, 2 vols. (Cambridge, MA: Harvard University Press, Belknap Press, 1981). These volumes contain photographic reproductions of all the poem manuscripts held by the Houghton College Library at Harvard. At present, no manuscript book exists for the large holding of Dickinson's poems at the Amherst College Library. It is through the courtesy of John Lancaster, the curator of Special Collections of the Frost Library and the Board of Trustees, Amherst College, that I reproduce the manuscript of "Knock with / tremor" and "Dear Father." Thanks are also due to Beth Kiley, Permissions Manager, Harvard University Press.

2. In discussing Emily Dickinson's parents with an eye toward the linguistic effects they might produce, I am deliberately violating

Lacan's imperative that one not translate concepts such as "Name-of-the-Father" into human terms. For Dickinson's life and writing illuminate Lacan's blindspot. Lacan has stated that the phallus is the signifier of a lack, of an irreducible gap between desire and the demand for desire's satisfaction. In his association of the lack with the Father and of a debased presence with the Mother, Lacan attempts to gender and circumscribe the power of dissemination. An effect of language, the phallus shatters the mother and child bond and the phallus becomes the elusive, impossible object of desire. But such a theory presumes that the mother's desire is *legible*. When the mother's desire is simulated or unreadable (as Derrida describes woman's effects in *Spurs*), the identity of the phallus is not unerringly reflected in her gaze. Lacanian psychoanalysis' account of language depends upon the mother's not being a *woman*, in the Nietzchean and Irigarayan sense of that term. When a mother is evasive, withholding, introspective, as Emily Norcross was, the power of the phallus is undermined. In *logos*, this mother represents the indeterminate possibility of fusion and interruption; she marks the spaces of silence between words in the father's discourse. Although Lacan attempts to totalize her in order to push her aside, as Emily Norcross reveals, the mother is the unstable in-between force in a paternal semantic system.

3. Revising Lacan, Julia Kristeva emphasizes the primacy of the pre-oedipal maternal discourse, the sensual rhythms and echolalias that the mother and infant use to communicate with each other. This bodily discourse is displaced and suppressed with the institution of language, or the symbolic realm associated with the Father's No which forbids possession of the mother's body. Yet the maternal discourse, or semiotic, persists within the symbolic, disrupting its progress. See Kristeva, "From One Identity to an Other," in *Desire in Language*, trans. Leon S. Roudiez (New York: Columbia University Press, 1980) 124-47; *Revolution in Poetic Language*, trans. Margaret Waller (New York: Columbia University Press, 1984); and "Stabat Mater," in *The Kristeva Reader*, ed. Toril Moi (New York: Columbia University Press, 1987). For a helpful overview of Lacanian theory, see Jacqueline Rose's introduction to *Feminine Sexuality: Jacques Lacan and the école freudienne* (New York: Norton, 1982), 27-57.

4 . The trope of *walking*, how to place one's (poetic) feet, is central to Dickinson's poetics, expressing her suspicion of a facile

"progress" in both its literary and cultural manifestations as well as her own ambivalence towards her "limping. " See (Journal 187) "How many times these low feet staggered—"; in "I can wade grief," the smallest drop of joy breaks up her feet (Journal 252). (Journal 512) "The soul has bandaged moments," where in her "retaken moments," she has "shackles on her plumed feet/ And staples—in her song." In "After great pain, a formal feeling comes—", "The Feet, mechanical, go round—" (Journal 341). In J. 792, "Through the strait pass of suffering— / The Martyrs—even—trod./ Their feet—upon Temptation— / Their faces—upon God—." In Journal 1760, "The accent of a coming Foot" marks the continguity of Elysium.

5. William Blackstone, *Commentaries on the Laws of England*, 4 vols. (1769; London: Dawsons of Pall Mall, 1966) 3: 279.

6. A powerful male authority 's ignoring a diminutive (presumably female) figure 's summons also occurs in J. 376, an early Dickinson poem. In manuscript, the poem's first seven lines appear as follows:

> Of Course—I prayed—
> And did God Care?
> He cared as much as
> on the Air
> A Bird—had stamped
> her foot
> And cried "Give Me"—

To represent a woman's unanswered prayer to a patriarchal deity, Dickinson compares herself to the Romantic figure for the poet, a Bird, stamping her uncapitalized and isolated "foot." According to the male authority, her poetry is noteless and insignificant, not worth responding to. Patriarchal neglect structures the primal scene for woman's writing. For a woman, this neglect figures *the* textual predicament.

7. On taking rhetorical questions literally, see Paul de Man, "Semiology and Rhetoric," *Allegories of Reading* (New Haven: Yale University Press, 1979) 3-19.

8. George Frisbie Whicher, *This Was a Poet: A Critical Biography of Emily Dickinson* (New York: Charles Scribner's Sons, 1939) 28-29.

9. *Emily Dickinson*, American Men of Letters Series (New York: William Sloane Associates, 1951) 12.

10. In his letter of June 4, 1828, Edward summarizes that she must possess "an amiable disposition—modest & unassuming manner—a thorough knowledge of every branch of domestic economy—good sense, cultivated & improved by a moderate acquaintance with a few of the most select works of taste, & an acquaintance & frequent intercourse with refined society & a happy contentment & equanimity of character, & a desire to promote the happiness of all around her." Two months later, having reached a "satisfactory conclusion respecting [Emily's] qualifications," Edward asks her to be his "friend for life" (quoted in Wolff, 37).

11. Sandra M. Gilbert and Susan Gubar, *No Man's Land: The Place of the Woman Writer in the Twentieth Century*, 3 vols. (New Haven: Yale University Press, 1988) 1: 265.

ELLEN LOUISE HART

# The Encoding of Homoerotic Desire: Emily Dickinson's Letters and Poems to Susan Dickinson, 1850-1886

During the last decade of Dickinson scholarship feminist critics have focused on Dickinson's relationships with other women, giving special attention to Susan Huntington Gilbert Dickinson, the poet's lifelong friend, sister-in-law, and neighbor, and the recipient of more of Dickinson's poems and letters than any other correspondent. Many critics today, feminists in particular, as well as those influenced by feminist criticism, read as love letters the affectionate, often passionate letters Dickinson sent Susan when both women were in their early twenties. Generally these critics accept that in the early 1850s Dickinson was in love with Susan. Most commonly assume, however, that a break in the friendship occurred in the late 1850s, sometime after Susan's marriage in 1856 to Dickinson's brother Austin, and they assert that the previously existing intimacy was never restored. In this essay I maintain that the love between the two women, best described as constant rather than stable, was a bond that never ended. Focusing on Dickinson's encoded language, I argue that the poet designs and inscribes a bond with Susan that she envisions as enduring even after death. Visions of reunion and a shared eternity originate in Dickinson's earliest writing to Susan, and yet most readers and critics ignore or misread this language. Drawing my evidence from poems and letters sent to Susan, I will focus here on a text that I read as a culminating moment in the life-long correspondence:[1]

> Morning
> might come
> by Accident—
> Sister—
> Night comes
> by Event—
> To believe the
> final line of
> the Card would
> foreclose Faith—
> Faith is *Doubt*—
>
>      Sister—
> Show me
> Eternity—and
> I will show
> you Memory—
> Both in one
> package lain
> And lifted
> back again—
>
> Be Sue—while
> I am Emily—
> Be next—what
> you have ever
> been—Infinity—
>
>      (letter 921)[2]

In reading "Morning," written in about 1884,[3] I will argue that the correspondence to Susan—especially the letters written after 1858—has been neglected and misread and that this particular text has been not only neglected, but mistakenly presented by Dickinson's editors solely as a letter and not also as a poem.

It is important to note that, as in any intimate, long-term relationship, there were periods of tension during the course of Dickinson's friendship with Susan and, particularly on Susan's part, times of rejection and neglect, but the hundreds of poems and letters Dickinson sent Susan from her early twenties until the last years of her life are testimony to the fact that Dickinson's love remained constant. Two years before her death, "constant" is the way Dickinson described herself as she concluded a letter to Susan: "Remember—Dear, an unfaltering Yes is my only reply to your utmost question—with constancy—Emily—" (letter 908). Misreading of the constancy and passion in this correspondence is due in part to the fact that while the early letters to Susan, often three to four pages in length, are generally discursive and descriptive, the later letters tend to be brief, sometimes no more than a line or two. The prose is often highly condensed, elliptic, enigmatic, and difficult to distinguish from poetry. It is a private language of love, and these letters and poems may be read as coded declarations of desire.

One letter written in 1882, when both women were fifty-two years old, reads: "Dear Sue—With the Exception of Shakespeare, you have told me of more knowledge than anyone living—To say that sincerely is strange praise—" (letter 757).[4] To contest that Shakespeare is among the living is a striking conceit and the comparison of Shakespeare and Susan is extraordinary. Like the writer to whom Dickinson most often referred, Susan provided knowledge of drama and passion.[5] Dickinson reminds Susan of their shared life, their deep and complex intimacy. The letter expresses awe and admiration, and yet is double-edged: its "strange praise" blames Susan for telling of, and causing, pain. Although we cannot determine its immediate circumstances, reading this letter in the context of the correspondence we find that the language has other points of reference. For example, two letters show that lines from Shakespeare's *Antony and Cleopatra* are used to allude to a special knowledge between the two women. Borrowing the voice of Mark Antony, Dickinson wrote to Susan when both women were forty-four, "'Egypt, thou knew'st'—" (letter 430), an allusion Susan would have understood:

> Egypt, thou knew'st too well,
> My heart was to thy rudder tied by the strings,
> And thou shouldst tow me after. O'er my spirit
> Thy full supremacy thou knew'st, and that
> Thy beck might from the bidding of the gods
> Command me.[6]

Nearly ten years later, Dickinson wrote again: "Susan's Calls are like Antony's Supper—'And pays his Heart for what his Eyes eat—only—'" (letter 854).[7]

These three letters speak a language of love and desire, but critics have overlooked this aspect of the later letters to Susan because the allusions are so condensed, because the playful tone in some of the letters can be misleading, and because many critics who assume a heterocentric point of view are led away from readings that recognize homoerotic passion. For many it has been impossible to conceive of erotic love between two adult women, between Dickinson, a poet who wrote passionately of men, and Susan, a wife and mother. They have difficulty accepting that Dickinson had intense romantic relationships with men at different times in her life, which coexisted with her lifelong attachment to Susan.[8] It may also be difficult for critics to see language between two women as marked by desire when the biography suggests that the relationship did not necessarily involve physical intimacy. Such is the power of the taboo against homoeroticism and so narrow the range of definitions of love in our culture.

In reading the text "Morning" as a love poem and understanding why it has been neglected, it is useful to consider how critics have historically read the correspondence to Susan and what views they have taken of the friendship. In 1937 George Frisbie Whicher, whose critical biography *This Was A Poet* became a standard text on Dickinson, described a break in the bond between the two women:

Insensibly they drifted further and further apart. Then a few notes would pass, sometimes extravagant in protests of affection, and there would be a momentary resumption of a relationship which rang more and more hollow. The one link between the two divided households was Austin's second son Gilbert, a true Dickinson and the darling of his father and his aunts alike, but when the enticing child died in 1883 the link was broken. The unfaltering yes that Emily once gave to Sue was tacitly revoked.[9]

Since the mid-1970s William Luce's "Belle of Amherst," on stage and on television, has echoed Whicher's position. In a dramatic monologue Dickinson "sadly" (stage directions) sums up the friendship as she looks from her bedroom window toward Susan's house next door and notes the "path between, just wide enough for two who love." This is a path no one uses any more, she says, a path she and Sue once used, Sue who understood her need to write but "didn't understand my love." She concludes: "The path is overgrown with weeds now. I guess it's best to abandon paths when you find they lead nowhere."[10]

That the path led nowhere is a line of thought extending itself to feminist criticism and to one of the most extensive studies to date on Dickinson's relationship with Susan. In *Dickinson: The Anxiety of Gender* Vivian Pollak devotes several chapters to Susan and gives one chapter her name. This is particularly notable since Richard Sewall in his two-volume biography makes a point of titling chapters for key figures but omits Susan from his titles and discusses her most fully in a chapter called "Early Hostilities."[11] In contrast to this kind of disparagement, Pollak reads the early correspondence to Susan insightfully. Exploring the homoeroticism in Dickinson's writing, Pollak is keenly sensitive to the predicament of a woman in the nineteenth century in love with another woman: "Although some feminist critics have suggested that homoerotic female friendships in nineteen-century America were easily reconciled with heterosexual commitments and untainted by guilt, for Dickinson the bonds of womanhood are more confining."[12] Yet eventually we find Pollak taking up the line, drawn by Whicher, carried on by Luce and many others, that the love for Susan had an end:

> Whereas Dickinson anticipates a heavenly reunion with her male lover in a significant cluster of poems, she *never anticipates a postmortem resurrection of her devastated sorority.* As a consequence, when her relationship to another woman is deadlocked, Dickinson's need to preserve her friendship is exceeded only by her desire to destroy it. To this end, she often introduces a symbolic male figure who relieves her of the burden of repudiating either her homosexual or her heterosexual identities. *This closure corresponds both to her inner necessity and to the historical conclusion of her relationship with Susan Gilbert Dickinson during the 1850s.*[13]

The emphasis is mine. As I will show, the later correspondence with Susan provides evidence that an "historical conclusion" did not take place and Dickinson did "anticipate a postmortem resurrection" with a woman.

Poet and critic Susan Howe objects to attempts to date the friendship's end: Susan Dickinson, she writes, "annuls fragile chronologies."[14] Focusing on the "libidinal freeing of the Imaginary Susan Gilbert" (p. 82) evoked in the poetry and on the "written condition of this relation," which she terms "leviathan," Howe writes, "every line touched down in ink or pencil on every scrap of paper sent to Susan Gilbert Dickinson inscribes a dialectic of infinite Desire" (p. 84). A line of lesbian critics, dating from Rebecca Patterson in 1951, has continued to explore Dickinson's "dialectic of infinite Desire" for women in general and for Susan in particular. But here, too, the emphasis is on the early correspondence. For Patterson, writing in the well-known *Riddle of Emily Dickinson* that the poet was in love with Susan during her early twenties, the later letters to Susan were not available. In the work of Lillian Faderman, whose *Surpassing the Love of Men* began as a study of Dickinson's love letters to Susan, the later letters are passed over.[15] The lesbian poet Judy Grahn does not specifically refer to the late correspondence, though significantly she does assert that Susan was "the mainstay love of the poet's life."[16] Grahn goes beyond Dickinson's life to a reading of Dickinson's vision of heaven, which would be "the joining of women" (p. 96)— "literally marriage beyond the grave" (p. 98).[17] My own position is closest to Grahn's: I will argue that through writing Dickinson designs territory beyond the grave, an eternity where she can locate and transform her lifelong love for Susan.[18]

"The incidents of / Love / Are more than / its' Events—" (poem 1248), Dickinson wrote to Susan. Their friendship is best documented and traced through poems and letters that both record and become "the incidents of Love." Still, a chronology of external "Events" is useful in piecing together the story of a love that "first began on the step at the front door, and under the Evergreens" (letter 177). Susan Huntington Gilbert was born in Greenfield, Massachusetts, on 19 December 1830, nine days after Dickinson's birth. Orphaned by the age of eleven, she was raised by an aunt in Geneva, New York until 1850, when she came to live with an older sister in Amherst. Dickinson probably met Susan when both girls were teenagers in the late 1840s and Susan came to visit her sister. The first letter she is known to have sent Susan derives from the winter of 1850. The letters she sent from the fall of 1851 to the summer of 1852 while Susan was in Baltimore teaching mathematics are desperate in their longing for her return. In 1853 she sent Susan one of the first poems she is known to have written. At about that time Dickinson's brother Austin began to show romantic interest in both Susan and her younger sister Martha. Dickinson seems first to have encouraged him in both pursuits, then when he began to pay more attention to Susan, to remind him of Martha's affections. When Dickinson found out that Austin and Susan had secretly become engaged, her letter to Austin uses the language of a defeated competitor: "Dear Austin, I am keen, but you are a good deal keener, I am *something* of a fox, but you are more of a hound! I guess we are very good friends tho', and I guess we both love [S]us[ie] just as well as we can" (letter 110).[19] Dickinson had little more to say about the engagement, which lasted for three years and seems to have been marked by tensions and lingering doubts on Susan's part. Dickinson's letters from 1854 and 1855 suggest that the women were spending much of their time together. In 1856 Susan married Austin, moving the wedding at the last minute from Amherst to Geneva, New York. Susan was vague about her reasons for the change, which seems to have kept the Dickinson family from attending the ceremony.

There are no letters to Susan from 1856. According to Thomas H. Johnson there are no letters to any correspondent from the year 1857; he finds a hiatus in the poetry from 1855 through 1857. There is no reason to believe that Dickinson stopped writing poetry for three years and then in 1858 wrote more than fifty poems.[20] While it is conceivable that Dickinson remained silent at the time of Susan's marriage, which is likely to have been a critical period of conflict and adjustment, it is also possible that correspondence to Susan, along with other work, has been lost or was destroyed.

After Susan and Austin were married, Austin began to practice law in Amherst, and the couple moved into the house call3ed the Evergreens, which Edward Dickinson had built next door. The correspondence resumes, and the longing for affection as well as the fear of rejection continue. In 1861 Susan's first child was born, and it appears that this event caused considerable anxiety for Dickinson, who seems to have feared that the baby would absorb too much of the new mother's attention. From this period one letter survives in which Susan responds as a critic to Dickinson's writing. In all probability Dickinson feared the loss of her most valued audience, whose comments on "Safe in their Alabaster Chambers" show her to have been an exacting reader of Dickinson's work. The exchange—Dickinson changed the poem and sent it back to Susan—shows respect, perhaps even dependence on Susan's tastes and judgment.[21]

There were signs of intermittent tension during the 1860s that perhaps were as much a result of the demands of Susan's position in Amherst social circles as of the demands of motherhood, but there is never a break in the flow of poems and letters sent to the house next door. With time Dickinson seems to have lost the fear she would be replaced by the children in Susan's affections; by the 1870s Dickinson was sending poems as gifts to the children and writing letters that show deep concern for their happiness and welfare. Occasionally these letters suggest that Dickinson thought of her niece and nephews as children she shared with Susan in an intimate way. In the summer of 1885 she wrote, "Dear Sue—I could send you no Note so sweet as the last words of your Boy—'You will look after Mother'?" (letter 999). There is no mention of Austin in these late letters. The failure of the marriage, the scandal of Austin's affair with Mabel Loomis Todd, a married woman and former friend of Susan's, are never mentioned, but are perhaps alluded to in tender messages to Susan consoling her for unnamed suffering.

Amherst rumours that, with the exception of the night of Susan's son Gilbert's death, after the late 1860s Dickinson no longer visited the house next door are probably true. The poet's letters indicate that Susan sometimes visited her and that Dickinson would not always answer the knock, once explaining later in a note: "You are too momentous" (letter 581). Events the women shared in these last years were exchanges of books, flowers, food. For Christmas in 1880 Susan inscribed a book: "Emily—Whom not seeing I still love—."[22] Suffering from kidney disease for the last two years of her life, Dickinson's final notes to Susan express appreciation for "solace." When Dickinson died Susan prepared the body for burial and chose flowers for the funeral. It is noteworthy that these intimate tasks were performed by Susan and not by Dickinson's sister, Lavinia. Evidence of Susan's deep and private grief is the note that accompanied the text of the obituary she wrote for *The Springfield Republican* asking the editor to "pardon untidiness for I am sick and weary."[23]

After Lavinia's discovery of the "packets" of poems, Susan's actions concerning their publication are puzzling.[24] Lavinia asked Susan to help with their transcription and editing, and at first Susan accepted, but after two years she withdrew, saying only that she did not think the poems would sell. Mabel Loomis Todd undertook the work, and Susan and Lavinia became increasingly estranged and hostile toward each other. During the 1890s Susan allowed several poems Dickinson had sent her to be published in periodicals, but these were not personal poems that would draw attention to her relationship with the poet.[25]

Following Susan's death in 1913, her daughter Martha Dickinson Bianchi brought out *The Single Hound: Poems of a Lifetime*, a collection of poems sent to Susan. During the last year of her mother's life, Bianchi tells us, Susan read and reread these poems and letters. Uncertain whether to burn them, she finally left the decision to her daughter who chose to produce "as a memorial to the love of these 'Dear, dead Women'" a volume that would introduce her mother as a central figure in the poet's life.[26] The opening sentence of her preface states, "The romantic friendship of my Aunt Emily Dickinson and her 'Sister Sue' extended from girlhood until death" (p. v).

How did Susan read these poems? What did they mean to her? Cristanne Miller in *Emily Dickinson: A Poet's Grammar* warns readers that since "Dickinson's practice of mailing the same poem in more than one letter is related to her practice of posing, . . . poems mailed in letters may be deceptively personal; they were not conceived solely in the light of a single friendship" (p. 13). Miller's point is well taken, but I want to draw a distinction between poems mailed in letters and poems mailed as letters. Many poems sent to Susan were not mailed in more than one letter. Most are addressed to her, and often the poem constitutes the entire text. Occasionally, especially in the later correspondence, the poem is part of the body of the letter; in these cases the poem lacks spaces or margins to indicate that it be read apart from the prose. Certainly there are poems Dickinson sent Susan that do not present themselves as personal poems. But I will argue here that poems of a personal nature addressed to Susan may be read as personal statements to her, as poems "conceived . . . in the light of a single friendship."

We have one example of a personal interpretation Susan may have given a poem she received from Dickinson. She concluded Dickinson's obituary with this stanza:

> Morns like these—we parted—
> Noons like these—she rose—
> Fluttering first—then firmer
> To her fair repose.

> (poem 27)

Here Susan takes on Dickinson's voice to describe Dickinson's resurrection. She uses lines that refer to the poet's system of symbolic time, in which "morning" represents the passage out of life and beyond, "noon" the time of resurrection. These lines constitute the first stanza of a poem found only in the packets; if Susan had received the entire poem, it is worth speculating on what the omitted lines might have meant to her:

> Never did she lisp it—
> It was not for me—
> She—was mute from transport—
> I—from agony—

> Till—the evening nearing
> One the curtains drew—
> Quick! A sharper rustling!
> And this linnet flew!

These stanzas show that "we" is not an unspecified plural, but signifies two, a bird who has flown and a bird excluded who longs to follow. Separation breaks their bond. The first bird is consumed by death and cannot "lisp," cannot share through even a crippled vocalization the experience of death's transfiguration. The linnet who remains is "mute from agony" until the approach of darkness, marked by curtains drawn by "one" left behind, who signifies the chain of human lives caught in a perpetual process of fear, separation, grief, and reunion. Death is not darkness; night is welcomed as an event that prefigures the linnet's passage. The linnet does not "flutter first, then firmer"; she soars toward her destination. The poem's ending is typical of Dickinson's teasing way of stopping short. But the decisiveness, the vitality of the final lines suggest that the linnet's goal is reached; the birds are reunited, their bond reestablished. Susan's use of this poem in the obituary may suggest that she had faith in and shared Dickinson's design—that when Dickinson died and in the language of the poem became the first bird to fly, Susan positioned herself as the bird who would follow.

"Unable are the / Loved—to die— / For Love is immortality— / Nay—it is Deity" (poem 809), Dickinson wrote to Susan in about 1865. The definition of love as deity operates consistently in the poetry, while the concept of God as deity is more problematic. Of the approximately three hundred poems Dickinson is known to have sent Susan, about a third are concerned with the questions: Does God exist? What will heaven be like? Will God "refund" "our confiscated Gods" (poem 1260), that is, will those we have loved on earth be returned to us in a life after death? Dickinson, who described her love of friends as "idolatrous," complained about the "jealous God" who "cannot bear to see / That we had rather not with Him / But with each other play" (poem 1719). Heaven was desired but uncertain; it was "the House of Supposition— / The Glimmering Frontier that / skirts the Acres of Perhaps," and her life on earth "this timid life of Evidence" that "keeps pleading—'I dont know'" (poem 696). Dickinson's ultimate preoccupation was not with God but with death and the things death would provide—resurrection and "Escape from Circumstances" (poem 382). Through poetry and the creation of a faith of her own, Dickinson escaped the circumstances of her separation from Susan.

The first poem Dickinson sent Susan in 1853, when both women were twenty-three years old, describes a journey on a "wondrous sea" (poem 4). Dickinson sent the poem to Susan with the heading: "Write! Comrade, write!" This heading exactly parallels a line in the first stanza: "Ho! Pilot, ho!" Although Dickinson uses conventional religious symbols throughout the poem—the "shore" where "no breakers roar," "the storm is o'er," "sails at rest" and "anchors fast"—the role of the pilot is unconventional. We might expect Jesus to be the pilot, but instead both women play the role each in turn. Susan is the comrade in life from whom Dickinson wants a letter, and in the poem Susan pilots the ship first as the two women set out together for the "peaceful west." With the line "Thither I pilot *thee*—" in the second stanza, Dickinson takes control of the ship as well as the idiom of the poem, and the sea voyage becomes a metaphor for desire and for death.

Another early poem sent to Susan begins in conventional ways to celebrate the sister next door: "One Sister have I in our house, / And one, a hedge away. / There's only one recorded, / But both belong to me" (poem 14). Susan is an outsider who has married into the family: she is the bird who built her nest among the Dickinson hearts and the bee who sings a different tune. The poem continues to present images that on the surface appear rather ordinary, for example, a vision of childhood: "up and down the hills / I held her hand the tighter— / Which shortened all the miles—." But this stanza begins, "Today is far from Childhood—," indicating that these sisters are women who hold hands and journey together, not children. Dickinson may be looking back on the friendship's past, an imagined view since there is no evidence that she knew Susan as a child, but this poem is not an elegy, as some critics have suggested. The poem looks forward to the friendship's unconventional future. As it does the image clusters become fragmented, the scene obscured:

And still her hum
The years among,
Deceives the Butterfly;
Still in her Eye
The Violets lie
Mouldered this Many May.

I spilt the dew—
But took the morn—
I chose this single star
From out the wide nights' numbers—
Sue—forevermore!

Susan's voice is the hum of the bee in competition with a butterfly for a flower; her eye beholds and consumes the flower
that, having passed on in time, is preserved through her
vision.[27] Dickinson is the flower who has "spilt the dew," who
has passed through morning in the day's cycle. She is a woman
who has sacrificed the sexual experience of early adulthood
and taken a different morn, choosing Susan as the star who
will lead her through the night into the morning of a shared
eternal life.

    After the late 1850s, the strategy of subverting conventional
images to describe Susan figures less in the poetry. However,
there is no abandonment of desire or expectation. The voice that
addresses Susan becomes increasingly direct. Sometimes it is
urgent and self-conscious, as in a poem sent in about 1863
headed "*Excuse* me—Dollie—" ("Dollie" was Susan's nickname).
In this poem Dickinson makes a desperate, passionate attempt to
define future possibility: "The Love a Child can / show—
below— / Is but a Filament—I / know / Of that Diviner—
Thing—" (poem 673). In this poem it is as if not only the "diviner
thing" but the vision itself were beyond reach of language. Verbs
are wildly grasped at to show what "This" can do:

        'Tis This—invites—appalls—
        endows—

Flits—glimmers—proves—
dissolves—
Returns—suggests—convicts—
enchants—
Then—flings in Paradise!

Love's power to attract and captivate, to materialize and disappear, to overwhelm with ecstasy occurs in and as a vision, and language, however limited, must satisfy.

Desperation never entirely leaves the poems. More often, however, especially in the poems after about 1860, the voice is intimate, tender, confident. Here is a stanza Dickinson sent in about 1863:

Ungained—it may
be
By a Life's low venture—
But then
Eternity enable the
endeavoring
Again—

(poem 680)

As readers outside this shared language, we identify "it" as the poem's "omitted center."[28] But to the initiated, that is, Susan, "it" represents the "fling" directed and made steady, the progression from love below, "Life's low venture," into eternity and paradise.

In 1872 Dickinson wrote to Susan:

Our own
possessions—
thought our own—
'Tis well to
hoard anew—
Remembering

the Dimensions
Of Possibility.

(poem 1208)

In 1880 on Susan's birthday she wrote:

Birthday of
but a single
pang
That there are
less to come—
Afflictive is
the Adjective
But affluent
the doom—

(poem 1488)

Both of these poems make use of a pattern of imagery common
in the poetry to Susan: hoarding and reclaiming a possession.
Susan is often represented as a gem or a precious metal, and
Dickinson may be "doomed" because the treasure can be taken
away by death or by the jealous God who is like a burglar.
But God also functions in the poetry as a "banker" who keeps
the treasure safe until it is reclaimed. Which role will God
finally play? This is unknown in Dickinson's scheme for eternal affluence. Her best answer—her strategy in the poems to
Susan—is to argue that "Remembering / the Dimensions / of
Possibility" requires faith.

In reading the poem "Morning," which is a declaration of
faith in possibility, it is useful to consider a definition of
"morning" Dickinson sent to Susan more than twenty years
earlier in about 1862:

"Morning"—means "Milking"
To the Farmer—
Dawn—to the Appenine—

Dice—to the Maid.
"Morning" means—just—Chance
To the Lover—
Just—Revelation—
To the Beloved—

(poem 300)

"Morning" means another chance to live: for the farmer it is the opportunity to earn a living, for the mountains it is the return of daylight. Morning means "dice" to the maid. To dice is to sew a decorative pattern of squares onto a piece of fabric; it may also refer to cooking; and it is a game of chance. To the maid and to the lover, morning is a chance to find love; to the beloved, it is the time when love's future will be revealed.

In the later poem to Susan, her "beloved," Dickinson reaffirms her faith in revelation.

Morning
might come
by Accident—
Sister—
Night comes
by Event—
To believe the
final line of
the Card would
foreclose Faith—
Faith is *Doubt*—

In the first stanza of the poem Dickinson attempts to reconcile belief in what can be known with faith in the unknowable. Inevitably death follows life, she tells Susan, as night follows morning in the day's cycle. "Morning" suggests its homonym "mourning," which might come "by Accident" if one of the women were suddenly to die. The question is whether the morning of new life is guaranteed or a matter of chance. Ultimately this is not a question of belief, but rather of faith, for "to believe the final line of the Card would foreclose Faith." The "Card" is the poem's most ambiguous image. It may refer to a message previously sent on a card or to a printed greeting card, a playing card, or a fortune telling card; it may represent a map or a chart since a circular piece of cardboard, marked with the points of a mariner's compass, is known as a card of the sea. The "Card" may even refer to the Bible, the "great card and compass" and guide to faith. Dickinson's own lexicon gives the following example of the word's usage, quoting Alexander Pope: "Reason the card, but passion is the gale."[29] This configuration bears the weight of the poem's central tensions: reason and belief are inadequate, yet they are all we have to guide and direct passion and faith. Belief in a final outcome dependent on chance constitutes a contradiction in terms, she argues, because belief would "foreclose" faith; it would both deprive faith of the equity of its own redemption and lay an exclusive claim to it.[30] But it is not necessary, or possible, for belief to cancel faith or monopolize it because doubt provides the context for faith; doubt measures the strength of commitment that faith demands and is itself the form in which faith continues.

This extraordinary logic marks a leap in faith and a leap in the poem, which appears physically as a break between stanzas. In the next stanza Dickinson offers the view of a shared past in exchange for Susan's vision of eternity:

> Sister—
> Show me
> Eternity—and
> I will show
> you Memory—
> both in one
> package lain
> And lifted
> back again—

The "package" in which both "Memory" and "Eternity" are lain may be the grave from which two bodies will be resurrected and transformed. "Package" may also signify the poems in which Dickinson has recorded her memory of the past and speculated on the future possibility of her life with Susan.

The poem "Morning" builds on contrasts: eternity, and Susan's power as the "beloved" to withhold or grant a future, and memory, Dickinson's power as a poet to recall and record the past. The poem pairs opposites that are actually complements—morning and night, faith and doubt, eternity and memory, finally leading us to the poem's central pair, "Sue" and "Emily":

> Be Sue—while
> I am Emily—
> Be next—what
> you have ever
> been—Infinity—

Here Dickinson requests that "Sue" and "Emily," whose lives have been both opposite and complementary, remain as they "have ever been," until, leaving their physical beings and individual identities, they join and merge in the "Costumeless Consciousness" (poem 1454) of immortality, of mind without body, without limit, free of artifice and the restrictions of gender. Finally, Dickinson asks that Susan continue as the link between faith and infinity, as the embodiment of a love whose equivalent is space and time devoid of all boundaries.

In exploring reasons why this poem has been excluded from the Dickinson canon and ignored, it is necessary to examine the different versions of the text as well as its publishing history. The poem was first published in 1924 by Martha Dickinson Bianchi in *The Life and Letters of Emily Dickinson*. Bianchi refers to the poem as a "pencilled message" and prints the text in the following form:

> Morning might come by accident, Sister,
> Night comes by event—

To believe the final line of the card
Would foreclose Faith,
Faith is doubt, Sister.
Show me Eternity, and
I will show you memory—
Both in one package lain
And lifted back again.
Be Sue while I am Emily,
Be next what you have ever been—
Infinity.[31]

In 1958 Thomas H. Johnson and Theodora Ward printed the poem as "letter 912":

Morning might come by Accident—Sister—
Night comes by Event—
  To believe the final line of the Card would foreclose Faith—
Faith is *Doubt.*
Show me Eternity, and I will show you Memory—
Both in one package lain
And lifted back again—
Be Sue—while I am Emily—
Be next—what you have ever been—Infinity—

It is remarkable that Johnson should represent "Morning" as he does and yet classify the poem as a letter.

Johnson has noted that it is not always possible with Dickinson's letters to distinguish when prose leaves off and verse begins. We need to ask what about this Dickinson text might mark it as a poem. The writing has the form of a poem: it appears in stanzas; it uses line divisions; and its lines are metered. The writing uses rhyme: "Accident" and "Event"; "Eternity" and "Memory"; "lain" and "again"; "Emily" and "Infinity." If we define a poem as two or more lines, which are rhymed or metered, use metaphorical language, and present themselves on the page in a way that draws special attention and separates them from other writing, are there any further texts that Johnson represents as poetry in his edition of the letters that he does not include in his variorum edition of the poems? I found four examples. The first is letter 117, signed "Emilie—Vinnie—":

A little poem we will write unto our Cousin John,
to tell him if he does not come and see us very soon,
we will immediately forget there's any such a man,
and when he comes to see us, we will not be "at home."[32]

It may be argued that this is a poem, but because it does not use symbolic language, it is not difficult to see why it might not be included in editions of the poetry. In letter 277 to Samuel Bowles, Johnson separates the last two lines from the text and prints them as poetry; in letter 411 he does the same with the last three lines. In neither case does he include the lines in his edition of the poems. In letter 735 to Thomas Wentworth Higginson, Johnson prints the last two lines as poetry, includes them in *The Poems* as poem 1512, but misses the preceding lines. The poem actually reads:

It is solemn to remember that Vastness—
Is but the Shadow of the Brain which casts it—
All things swept sole away
This—is immensity—[33]

I think these omissions are simply mistakes.

Johnson's omission of "Morning" may have been mistaken, or perhaps he misread the poem. Exactly how and why would he have misread it? It is not likely that he considered the text too personal since there are many examples of letters also included as poems that focus on an incident or event in the life of a friend. For example, poem 222/letter 208 was occasioned by a gift of garters to Kate Scott Anthon: "When Katie walks, this simple pair accompany her side." Poem 218/letter 232 followed the birth of Susan's first child: "Is it true, dear Sue? / Are there *two*?" It is also unlikely that the character of the poem as a message afforded reason for its omission. In his notes to *The Poems* Johnson often calls a poem a "note in verse" or a "letter poem." For example, one "letter poem" (poem 1515) to Mrs. Holland begins:

The Things that never can come back, are several—
Childhood—some forms of Hope—the Dead—
Though Joys—like Men—may sometimes make a Journey—
And still abide—

These lines are prosaic; they are without the highly condensed language we often find in a Dickinson poem. But Johnson does not identify the text as prose and exclude it from *The Poems*.

Johnson took many liberties with texts. For example, he printed poem 1637 as a four-line stanza, but when he published the same text as a letter, he arranged the lines in the following manner:

Is it too late to touch you, Dear?

We this moment knew—
Love Marine and Love terrene—
Love celestial too—

(letter 975)[34]

Dickinson's text does not use spacing to distinguish between verse and prose. In Johnson's note on the poem he remarks: "It is impossible in such a *jeu d'esprit* to be sure where the prose leaves off and the poetry begins, a situation that in many instances ED seems to have intended."[35] With this text Johnson is touched by "*jeu d'esprit*." It would appear that in poems to women he found wit moving and illuminating, not passion.

Johnson calls poem 1401/letter 531 a "note" and includes it in the poems:

To own a Susan of my own
Is of itself a Bliss—

> Whatever Realm I forfeit, Lord,
> Continue me in this!

The light and playful tone makes this poem appear transparent. "Own," "Bliss," and "Realm," however, are key words in the symbolic language Dickinson used in writing to Susan, and these words have resounding meanings—possession, passion, eternal life. This is not a language Johnson shared. He was unfamiliar with it, and he may have been uncomfortable with it. At times he sounds almost prescriptive concerning Susan's role as wife and mother: "[Dickinson's] correspondence with Susan Gilbert necessarily altered its character after Susan's marriage to Austin in July 1856,"[36] and "In 1861 the first child of Austin and Susan Dickinson was born, an event that engrossed Sue's attention. The continued exchange of notes with Sue thereafter is warm but never urgent."[37] It is important to consider how such a reading of the correspondence to Susan may have affected its editing.

Richard Sewall has written of "explaining, if not explaining away, the fervor of the letters."[38] Johnson would appear to be "explaining away" by attaching poems of particular power and intimacy to special occasions. Unless a poem or letter was postmarked, dated, or connected to some known event, which not many of them were, all dating is ultimately speculative. And yet Johnson suggests that "One Sister have I in our house" was occasioned by Susan's birthday. "Birthday of but a single pang" was "evidently" ("probably" is the word he used later in *The Letters*) sent to Susan on her fiftieth birthday. It is as if Johnson were looking for ways to explain passion away by attributing poems to ceremonial moments in the friendship. Finally, it is possible that Johnson considered "Morning" unreadable except to its recipient. He may have found "the final line of the Card," the poem's most oblique references, incomprehensible. Still this would not explain why he did not choose to print the text as a poem, while mentioning its difficulty for the reader and adding the note he sometimes used: "The occasion for this poem is not known."

In the end it is impossible to know why we do not have this text among Dickinson's poems. Only the effect of its neglect can be calculated. In linking names—"Be Sue while / I am Emily"—the poem omits no center, to use Jay Leyda's term:

> A major device of Emily Dickinson's writing, both in her poems and in her letters, was what might be called the "omitted center." The riddle, the circumstance too well known to be repeated to the initiate, the deliberate skirting of the obvious—this was the means she used to increase the privacy of her communication; it has also increased our problems in piercing that privacy.[39]

"Morning" pierces an aspect of Dickinson's privacy. But as long as this poem is not available to students, teachers, and general readers, as long as scholars and critics relegate the text to the categories "insignificant" and "unreadable," one more piece of evidence that Dickinson loved Susan all her life and designed a future in which to extend and transform that love is removed from view. Christopher Benfey has written that Dickinson criticism seems constantly to be beginning. As the entire correspondence to Susan reaches more readers; as the text of "Morning" is recovered and readings of the poem are informed by an awareness of Dickinson's lifelong desire for Susan; as the pattern of omitting or undermining materials concerning the poet's love for women is broken, a pattern so damaging to Dickinson scholarship for so long, Dickinson criticism will begin once again.

## Notes

An earlier version of this essay was presented in 1987 at the Feminist Studies Focused Research Activity Spring Quarter Conference at the University of California at Santa Cruz. I would like to thank the following people for their support: Michael Cowan and Helene Moglen at UCSC for reading the earliest drafts; Tilly Shaw at UCSC who read drafts repeatedly, and contributed substantially to the essay's development; Vivian Pollak for her generous encouragement; George Crawford and Dr. Ann Rittenhouse for their Boston hospitality; and James McMullen of Now What Software for the invaluable gift of a personal computer. I would also like to acknowledge the Houghton Library, Harvard University, for permission to quote from the Dickinson Collection.

1. Dickinson sent Susan close to three hundred extant poems and approximately one hundred and fifty letters. Three letters from Susan remain; presumably others were destroyed as a result of Dickinson's request at the time of her death that the letters in her possession be burned.

2. I quote reference numbers for each poem and letter using the numbering systems established in *The Poems of Emily Dickinson*, ed. Thomas H. Johnson, 3 vols. (Cambridge: Harvard University Press, 1955), and in *The Letters of Emily Dickinson*, ed. Thomas H. Johnson, 3 vols. (Cambridge: Harvard University Press, 1958). However, unless otherwise noted, all Dickinson texts for which holographs exist are quoted from original manuscripts or photostats at the Houghton Library, or from Ralph Franklin, *The Manuscript Books of Emily Dickinson* (Cambridge: Harvard University Press, 1981). Therefore, orthography, punctuation, spacing, and lineation in texts represented here will often be at variance with the versions that appear in Johnson's editions and with almost all other print representations of the poems. The line divisions in Dickinson's poems are currently being contested. See Susan Howe's debate with Ralph Franklin, who maintains that line breaks are a matter of "arbitrary convenience"; Howe argues that the line breaks are intentional visual strategies, in "Visual Intentionality in Emily Dickinson," *HOW(ever)* 3, no. 4 (1986): 11-13.

3. I use Johnson's dates for poems and letters advisedly; because Dickinson dated so little of her writing, much of the dating of her work ultimately must be speculative.

4. This is the entire letter. The next letter referred to, Letter 430, is also quoted in its entirety.

5. For a discussion of the frequency of Dickinson's references to Shakespeare, see Jack L. Capps, *Emily Dickinson's Reading: 1836-1886* (Cambridge: Harvard University Press, 1966).

6. William Shakespeare, *The Tragedy of Antony and Cleopatra*, in *The Complete Plays and Poems of William Shakespeare*, eds. William Allan Neilson and Charles Jarvis Hill (Cambridge: Houghton Mifflin, 1970), III. xi. 56-61.

7. *Antony and Cleopatra*, II. ii. 230-31. This letter is not quoted in full. In *The Riddle of Emily Dickinson* (Boston: Houghton Mifflin, 1951), a study that was ground breaking in its focus on Dickinson's erotic relationships with women (with Susan but more particularly with Susan's friend Kate Scott Anthon) and yet flawed by the inaccessibility of the poet's complete works at that time, Rebecca Patterson notes Dickinson's use of *Antony and Cleopatra* in letter 430; see p. 98. In *Emily Dickinson's Imagery*, ed. Margaret H. Freeman (Amherst: The University of Massachusetts Press, 1979), Patterson expands on her discussion of the Antony and Cleopatra references; see pp. 154-55.

Camille Paglia in her problematic study of Dickinson as a "male genius and visionary sadist," advancing her sensational view of the poet's "voyeurism, vampirism, necrophilia, lesbianism, sado-masochism, sexual surrealism" (p. 673), identifies "the stormy thirty-five-year relationship" with Susan as a "love affair" (p. 670) and reads letter 430 as a sign of tension and of Dickinson's willingness to play "humiliated Antony to Susan's Cleopatra" (p. 671). See chapter 24, "Amherst's Madame de Sade: Emily Dickinson," in *Sexual Personae: Art and Decadence from Nefertiti to Emily Dickinson* (New Haven: Yale University Press, 1990).

8. The most famous examples of Dickinson's passionate letters to a man are letters 187, 233, and 248 (tentatively placed in the period from about 1858 to about 1862), the so-called "Master letters," written to an unknown recipient and perhaps never sent. In addition to Johnson's *Letters*, see Franklin's manuscript edition *The Master Letters of Emily Dickinson* (Amherst: Amherst College Press, 1986). Other correspondences with men which suggest romantic attachments include her letters to Samuel Bowles (1858-77) and to Itis Lord (1878-83). A number of love poems refer to "Master," "Sir," "Sire," or use the masculine pronoun; see poems 96, 106, 246, 296, 336, 366, 461. Poems 446 and 494 are written in two versions, one with masculine and one with feminine pronouns.

9. George Frisbie Whicher, *This Was a Poet: A Critical Biography of Emily Dickinson* (Philadelphia: Dufour Editions, 1952), 35.

10. William Luce, *The Belle of Amherst* (Boston: Houghton Mifflin, 1976), 30.

11. Richard Sewall, *The Life of Emily Dickinson* (New York: Farrar, Straus, Giroux, 1974), I, 161-69.

12. Vivian R. Pollak, *Dickinson: The Anxiety of Gender* (Ithaca: Cornell University Press, 1984), 145.

13. Ibid., 137.

14. Susan Howe, "Women and Their Effect in the Distance," *Ironwood* 28 (1986): 84. Further citations will appear in the text.

15. Lillian Faderman, *Surpassing the Love of Men: Romantic Friendship and Love Between Women from the Renaissance to the Present* (New York: William Morrow, 1981).

16. Judy Grahn, *The Highest Apple: Sappho and The Lesbian Poetic Tradition* (San Francisco: Spinsters Ink, 1985), 141. Grahn notes that this conclusion is the result of her private conversations with Dickinson scholar Paula Bennett whose work on Dickinson includes "The Language of Love: Emily Dickinson's Homoerotic Poetry," *Gai Saber* 1, no. 1 (1977): 13-17, and *My Life a Loaded Gun: Female Creativity and Feminist Poetics* (Boston: Beacon Press, 1986). Further references to Grahn will appear in the text.

17. This survey of critics who have contributed to the study of Dickinson's correspondence with Susan is exemplary rather than exhaustive. See also Adalaide Morris, "'The Love of Thee—a Prism Be': Men and Women in the Love Poetry of Emily Dickinson," in *Feminist Critics Read Emily Dickinson*, ed. Suzanne Juhasz (Bloomington: Indiana University Press, 1983), no. 3 (1987): 3-25; Smith examines the silences imposed on the relationship, focusing on Austin and Mabel Loomis Todd's mutilations of the manuscripts and attempts to delete references to Susan.

Cristanne Miller in *Emily Dickinson: A Poet's Grammar* (Cambridge: Harvard University Press, 1987) takes a cautious stand on the relationship: as she moves from a discussion of an 1878 letter to a letter written twenty-five years earlier, she states that at this time Dickinson was "apparently in love with Sue" (p. 16); still, Miller's first chapter, "Letters to the World," is useful in orienting readers to Dickinson's use of her poems in letters and in helping sensitize readers to the poet's "gendered possibilities of meaning" (p. 17). Further references to Miller will appear in the text.

Recent biographies by Christopher Benfey, *Emily Dickinson: Lives of a Poet* (New York: George Braziller, 1986), and Helen McNeil, *Emily Dickinson* (New York: Virago/Pantheon Pioneers, 1986), emphasize Dickinson's early love for Susan; however, Benfey takes the position that relations with Susan were "often strained" (p. 22), and McNeil finds that Susan "had once been Emily's closest friend" (p. 34). Cynthia Griffin Wolff's biography, *Emily Dickinson* (Reading, Massachusetts: Addison-Wesley, 1988) does not identify the friendship with Susan as a love relationship. Bettina L. Knapp, in *Emily Dickinson* (New York: Continuum, 1989), questions whether Dickinson considered herself a third party in Austin and Susan's marriage and wonders if the poet viewed them "as fulfilling the role of parents that her own had so inadequately played?" (p. 44). Knapp's strategy for speculating on what she identifies as "an intense and mysterious love relationship" (p. 41) is to open up the matter, then leave it hanging, through the use of rhetorical questions: "Did she believe that, after her brother's marriage, the love bond she now enjoyed with Susan could possibly continue after marriage?" (p. 41). "What kind of passion had Sue fostered in Emily's heart, in those inner rooms and corridors of her mansion/brain?" (p. 182).

18. In examining Dickinson's vision of heaven it is useful to consider the work of her contemporary Elizabeth Stuart Phelps, whose immensely popular novel *The Gates Ajar* (Boston: Fields, Osgood, and Company, 1869) chronicles the course of a young woman's grief for her brother lost in the Civil War. Phelps tells the story of the despairing Mary's spiritual transformation through the help of her Aunt Winifred, who has lost her husband but lives confident in the knowledge that they will be reunited and live again in heaven *exactly* as they have lived together on earth. Phelps' heaven, which she continued to describe in two later works, *Beyond the Gates* (Boston: Houghton Mifflin, 1883) and *The Gates Between* (Boston: Houghton Mifflin, 1887), is a place where people see and touch each other and maintain blissful daily lives surrounded by their loved ones. We do not know if Dickinson had read Phelps—the Dickinson family did own a work of her mother's, Elizabeth Stuart Phelps (Phelps wrote under her mother's name after her mother died in 1852). The tremendous popularity of *The Gates Ajar* would attest to

the fact that Dickinson lived in a time marked by the need for domesticating religion and literalizing the figure of heaven. Although Dickinson's representation of immortality is more often a condition of unending consciousness and less like Phelps' vision of a detailed landscape, *The Gates Ajar* speaks to Dickinson's concerns about reunion after death with those she loved.

19. The manuscript of this letter has been mutilated; for a discussion of the partial erasure of "Susie," see Smith, p. 8.

20. Again, it is important to note that Johnson's dating cannot always be accurate.

21. See Johnson's notes to poem 216, I, 151-55.

22. *Endymion*, by The Earl of Beaconsfield (London: D. Appleton and Company, 1880), is in the Dickinson collection at the Houghton Library, Harvard University.

23. This manuscript is among Susan Dickinson's papers at the Houghton Library, Harvard University.

24. I use the term "packets" because it is a common, colloquial term that could arise out of Dickinson's vernacular; others use "fascicles" or "manuscript books" to describe the units of poems Dickinson copied onto stationery, sewed together, and preserved. We have no way of knowing how she might have referred to them.

25. Dickinson's sister held the rights to the poetry and ordered Susan to stop publishing poems in her possession. Lavinia died in 1899, but Susan allowed nothing further to be published during her lifetime.

26. Emily Dickinson, *The Single Hound: Poems of a Lifetime*, ed. Martha Dickinson Bianchi (Boston: Little, Brown, 1915), vi. Further references will appear in the text.

27. Generally in the poetry both bee and butterfly are figures that pursue liberty and sensuality.

28. This is a phrase Jay Leyda uses in *The Years and Hours of Emily Dickinson* (New Haven: Yale University Press, 1960), xxis. Further references will appear in the text.

29. Dickinson's lexicon is in the Dickinson collection at the Houghton Library, Harvard University.

30. *The Compact Edition of the Oxford English Dictionary* (Oxford University Press, 1971) gives as one meaning for "foreclose": "*Law of Mortgage* . . . to deprive of the equity of redemption." (Use of legal terms is characteristic of Dickinson whose father and brother were both lawyers.) Another meaning given for "foreclose" is "to establish an exclusive claim to." The *OED*'s example of this usage is taken from an address by Dickinson's contemporary Ralph Waldo Emerson, in *OED*, I, 1052.

31. Martha Dickinson Bianchi, *The Life and Letters of Emily Dickinson* (Boston: Houghton Mifflin, 1924), 87.

32. All of the poems quoted in this discussion of Johnson's editing use Johnson's versions of the text rather than the manuscripts.

33. Here I have finished constructing the quatrain using Johnson's pattern of lineation.

34. This poem was sent to Mary Warner Crowell in 1885.

35. Johnson, *Poems*, III, 1122.

36. Johnson, *Letters*, II, 314.

37. Johnson, *Letters*, II, 332.

38. Sewall, I, 163.

39. Leyda, p. xxi.

DAVID W. HILL

# Words Doing: Dickinson's Language as Autonomous Action

> The chickens grow very fast—
> I am afraid they will be so large
>      that you cannot perceive them
> with the naked eye when you get home.
>          . . . . . . . . . . . . . . . . .
> The cat walking down the stair
> makes a great noise—the banister
> bulges out as she descends. . . .
>
> Lewis Turco, "The Naked Eye" 1-4, 13-15

Emily Dickinson's stance toward the poem is "This is happening, and it is happening now." Her writing is neither the journalism of Whitman ("I was there and saw this happen"), nor the usual, assisting, inciting role of Emerson ("This is what will happen if you take some steps to see what I think I have seen"). That stance toward the poem grows out of a stance toward the language-events which happened to her so often. When she was twelve, the absence of her brother Austin evoked, in the first of her letters to be published, the language-play Lewis Turco drew from to start his poem "The Naked Eye" (*New Book of Forms*, 65). Her observation, and the one of Turco's with which I pair it above led me to the following question: What happens after word-events occur to Emily Dickinson? What does she do with them in letters and poems?

A lot has been written about the theories of representation readers can infer from her work, but the hypothesis I want to start with is simple: Dickinson looks out from those moments of language as if they were doors or windows. Of course, in her verse she often processed such language occurrences into figures of speech—ornaments, perhaps—and into figures of thought—maybe button-buttonhole mechanisms which fasten things together for a while. But her particular stance toward the "processing" of the words that happen to one differs from the kind of attitude toward language one finds in other writers. The transactions writers and readers are accustomed to carry out with each other occur in Dickinson in a very different mode.

It is tempting to infer that—thus young—Dickinson precociously shared with her brother an instance of the characteristic figure of thought we discuss in the word "circumference." The naked eye cannot see or contend with the sheer "it-ness" of a nature whose fecundity produces über-fowl in the Dickinson backyard. Something a little like that might have happened to Turco when he made his wonderful observation about the sheer presence of family cats stumping down stairs, but in her letter Dickinson seems to me more interested in the chickens than in the image for its own sake. The twelve-year-old acted like a conventional letter-writer, it seems to me, using the image of the chickens as a figure of speech that ornaments intensifies—the picture of growth she drew for her absent brother. But even in 1842, the language-event happened, whether she did very much with it or not.

Gary Lee Stonum named the quality which for me captures the stance as a poet and letter-writer that for me defines Dickinson's characteristic mode. He cites an 1878 note to Susan Gilbert Dickinson:

. . . . . . . . . . . . . . . .

Cherish Power—dear—
Remember that stands in the Bible between
    the Kingdom and the Glory,

because it is wilder than either of them.

(letter 583,[1] quoted in Stonum,53)

Language has power because words are so "wild"—wild enough to provide a counterweight to chickens who wax so terrifyingly huge.

Exterior wildness—bad weather—produced another language-event of some interest . In a letter to her again-departed brother Austin, nine years after the family chickens became so enormous, the 21-year-old Dickinson devastatingly outlined the parlor-life of a gloomy family whose portrayed stolidity and sheer *wontedness* must have been as soothing and satisfying to the departed Austin as the memory of ancestral pot-roasts:

> Our state is pretty comfortable, and our feelings are *somewhat solemn* which we account for satisfactorily by calling to mind the fact that it is the "Sabbath Day." Whether a certain passenger in a certain yesterday's stage has any sombre effect on our once merry household, or the reverse "I dinna choose to tell," but be the case as it may, we are a rather crestfallen company to make the *best* of us, and what with the sighing wind, the sobbing rain, and the whining of nature *generally*, we can hardly contain ourselves, and I only hope and trust that your this evening's lot is cast in far more cheery places than the ones you leave behind.
>
> We are enjoying this evening what is called a "northeast storm"—a little north of east, in case you are pretty definite. Father thinks "it's amazin raw," and I'm half disposed to think that he's in the right about it, tho' I keep pretty dark, and dont *say* much about it! Vinnie is at the instrument, humming a pensive air concerning a young lady who thought she was "almost there." Vinnie seems much grieved and I really suppose *I* ought to betake myself to weeping; I'm pretty sure that I *shall* if she dont abate her singing.

Father's just got home from meeting and Mr Bolt-
wood's, found the last quite comfortable, and the first not
quite so well.

Mother is warming her feet, which she assures me
confidently are "just as cold as ice.["] I tell her I fear there
is danger of identification, or ossification dont know certainly which! Father is reading the Bible—I take it for *consolation*, judging from outward things. He and mother
take great delight in dwelling upon your character, and
reviewing your many virtues, and Father' s prayers for
you at our morning devotions are enough to break one's
heart—it is really very touching; surely "our blessings
brighten" the farther off they fly! Mother wipes her eyes
with the end of her linen apron, and consoles herself by
thinking of several future places "where congregations
ne'er break up," and Austin's have no end! This being a
favorite sentiment with you, I trust it will find a response
in all patriotic bosoms. There has not been much stirring
since when you went away ' I should venture to say *pru-
dently* that matters had come to a stand—unless something new "turns up" I cannot see anything to prevent a
*quiet season*. Father takes care of the doors, and mother of
the windows, and Vinnie and I are secure against all outward attacks. If we can get our *hearts "under"* I dont have
much to fear—I've got all but *three* feelings down, if I can
only keep them! (letter 42)

The letter is still conventionally transactive, and a very good
letter for a brother just away from the family circle; Dickinson
paints a scene and tells a story probably of great attractive-
ness to the just-escaped, just-bereft Austin. "What with the
sighing wind, the sobbing rain, and the whining of nature *generally*," is a phrase which opens the scene-painting proper;
those last five words reveal the Dickinsonian power. Vinnie
may "sigh," Mother, may in her way "sob," but "whining generally" captures the parlor-weather as well as the cold June
rainstorm. What sets off the letter for me is deftly established

tone—Dickinson the under-stater—and its framing by the picture of "whining" nature. While some motifs from the poems of the 1860s and 70s appear in grub-state—"surely 'our blessings brighten' the further off they fly!" (poem 1209, for example); "several future places 'where congregations ne'er break up,' and Austins have no end," "[i]f we can get our *hearts* '*under*'"—they are not taken up. Like the weather, they serve the social purpose of the letter, a purpose which in these times many critics might identify as ulterior to the play of language.

There are, however, degrees and kinds of ulteriority. What I encounter in much Dickinson—and what Turco responded to—is neither statement ornamented with wit nor figures of thought—though the poems and letter are rich with both. There is not an overtly *ulterior* dimension—a plane of reference—into which Dickinson's moments of language happening are insistently set or which they insist upon inciting. They themselves are the central events of the poem—this is happening, and happening *now*.[2]

An illustrative example is the contrast between Emerson's use of his observations in "The Snow-Storm" and Dickinson's "It sifts from leaden sieves" (311).[3] In "The Snow-Storm" Emerson records some language which sets off parallel observations in Dickinson—"seems nowhere to alight," "tumultuous privacy of storm," "unseen quarry evermore furnished," "mad wind's night-work." But even as he recorded the language which creates these observations, Emerson put them into an ulterior scene, dramatizing the power of nature to isolate, hinting at the compensations of "tumultuous privacy," evoking the helplessness of the sighing farmer, and then deftly playing the master-chord of much of his writing—the assertion that we are "connate"[4] with a nature which seems to overwhelm us, but which, in its "frolic architecture," evokes the designs we strive so slowly to produce. We are overwhelmed by the storm which, while it seems "nowhere to alight," swallows our purposes and powers. But Emerson takes control over the poem even as storm masters the landscape; the storm is "artificer," mason, architect, whose forms parallel those human ones, "built in an age." The energy is untamed by "number or pro-portion." Proprieties are flouted in the onrush of energy, which leaves art "astonished," but demonstrates again the common roots of self and nature.[5]

That Dickinson thought of Emerson's poem is clear from the echoes—veil, artisans, ruffling post-wrists, and in the apparently earlier 1862 draft, swans.[6] But what she did with those observations reveals the particular quality of her atti-tude toward language. The tone and *singleness* of the Dickinson make the energy and populatedness of the Emerson poem seem by contrast to be foot-lights which convert the private moment of the snow into another stage on which Emerson can rewrite the gospel of our connate relation to nature. As she traces the burying of life in the snow, its fanciful shapes, and its marvellous disappearance, Dickinson evokes the experience which Emerson subordinates to his "ulterior" interest in the drama of our discovery that nature unfolds shapes parallel to those we unfold in our own consciousness.

While "The Snow-Storm" *does* something, the Dickinson poem *is* something; it evokes a state. The poem incites inter-pretation but does not insist upon a particular interpretive direction. Several of her observations—the evening out of dis-tinctions in the landscape (5-8), the "veiling" of the remnants of an otherwise "recordless" harvest (12-16),[7] the separation of "it" from the snow-storm, and the denial by "it" of the exis-tence of "its Artisans" (19)—seem to assert, but the assertion is incomplete, not part of a predication. Her later revisions of the poem (in 1864, copied out with two small changes in 1883) seem to me particularly striking. She denies the occasions for interpretation I cited above. After the first four lines she sub-stitutes these "stative" lines:

> It scatters like the Birds
> Condenses like a Flock
> Like Juggler's Flowers situates
> Upon a baseless Arc—
> It traverses—yet halts—

Disperses, while it stays
Then curls itself in Capricorn
Denying that it was—[8]

Whatever the status of the revision, it is clear that there is no taking up of the inferred context I and other readers find in the poem. She evokes the *state* of seeing a snow-storm and responding to its features of evanescence, its seeming "nowhere to alight," as Emerson has it. It is as if she observes the dynamics of snow-flakes in the fluid medium of air and that event, that observation out of which Emerson made much, is for Dickinson sufficient. In the 1862 versions, the establishment of an "it" outside the storm permits the inferential creation of a "scene" in which the reader can treat the snow-storm as Longfellow did in "Snow-Flakes," where the storm becomes the expression of a gloomy thought, even the 1862 Dickinson poem resides in the sense-experience and its extensions.

Even as Emerson recorded his wonderful language-events, he placed them into contexts, often the ministering contexts of his professional and moral life as a person called to give sermons and lectures. His experiences of his own language were always engaged, and he thought of words as ministers of a *Word* beyond them. An entry in his 1839 journals, while he still occasionally preached, establishes the homiletic base which makes his language use almost always *interested*:

At Church today I felt how unequal is this match [Emerson marked out the word "war" here] of words against things. Cease, o thou unauthorized talker, to prate of consolation, & resignation, and spiritual joys, in neat & balanced sentences. For I know these men who sit below, & on the hearing of these words look up. Hush quickly; for care & calamity are things to them. There is Mr. Tolman the shoemaker, whose daughter is gone mad, and he is looking up through his spectacles to hear what you can offer for his case. Here is my friend, whose scholars are all leaving him, & he knows not what to turn his hand to, next. Here is my wife who has come to church in hope of being soothed & strengthened after being wounded by the sharp tongue of a slut in her house. Here is the stage driver who has the jaundice, & cannot get well. Here is B. who failed last week, and he is looking up. O speak things, then, or hold thy tongue. (*JMN* 7:197)

*Things* to be spoken are personal, spiritual, social realities which the utterer must recognize as communicable help to another. Words are ministers which do work by conveying realities, here consolatory or advisory, to people in need of them.

There is an impulse to service I find at work in Emerson's responses to the most radical experiences of the kind of language he called "the metamorphosis." A particular striking example is the passage in "The Poet," in which he takes delight in Swedenborg's sense of language as metamorphic:

Certain priests, whom he describes as conversing very learnedly together, appeared to the children, who were at some distance, like dead horses; and many the like misappearances. And instantly the mind inquires, whether these fishes under the bridge, yonder oxen in the pasture, those dogs in the yard, are immutably fishes, oxen, and dogs, or only so appear to me. . . . We have all seen changes as considerable in wheat and caterpillars. He is the poet, and shall draw us with love and terror, who sees, through the flowing vest, the firm nature, and can declare it. (*Collected Works* 3:21)

The sacralization of organic nature is the guarantor for Emerson of the stability of the universe, and of the limits on the "wildness" of words. The "metamorphosis," no matter how strange in its appearance, is merely another instance of the familiar process of germination. The "things" expressed in this passage are not doctrines in the sense of conventional dogmas, but they establish a transactional context. Priests who are dead horses can be made to speak to people in need of comfort and understanding that there are "things" behind the words.

A Dickinsonian analogue is "This World is not Conclusion" (501). The *thing* which "narcotics" such as "Much Gesture, from the Pulpit" or "Strong Hallelujahs" cannot "still" is not simply the dogma stated in the first sentence. It is not a poem about the afterlife. Instead it is a dramatization, among other things, of what it is like to be in a congregation smarter than its preacher, who apparently does not know the need to "speak things." The moment of striking language in the poem—lines 2-4—would be as coy as the coquettish personification of faith in lines 13-15 if it were not the ground for the whole business.

> A species stands beyond—
> Invisible as Music—
> But positive as Sound—

This is processed, figured language in which the synesthesia typical of the language-events which happened to Dickinson has been made into ground of a discourse between the "conventional" modes (the least interesting of which is gesture- and hallelujah-filled religiosity) offered to the seeker and the elusive, unstated, evanescent window-opening which creates that fluttering instant of certainty unavailable to those who try to drug the tooth with the narcotics of ideational, emotional, or dogmatic structures of certainty. The striking, Dickinson quality is to see that window-opening in words. What she does with it is to establish a tone for understanding human reaction, as she did with the whining weather in the 1851 letter.

Emerson feels responsible, while Dickinson's poem dramatizes an orthodox church-service as a charmingly irrelevant, comically crude attempt to build a structural and long-lasting scaffolding around something which is certain only because it is so elusive. Her poem of alleged statement does state something that grows out of the dogma in the first line.

However, the statement is neither teaching nor a journalist's look back. Instead, it wryly evokes the comical possibilities of original sin conceived of as the human embarrassment of lacking sufficient emotional or intellectual equipment to make anything very useful out of what others immure in the doctrine of grace. While interesting inferred interpretations of the poem abound, one speculates on what Emerson's reaction would have been were he to have had a listener in the pews below him so intelligently alert to the inequality of "match" between the language of religiosity and the *things* of religious perception. The "things" he felt compelled to offer his congregation and his readers were from the "slow-structure," "stone-by-stone" side of himself, while Dickinson rested in her linguistic equivalent of "the mad wind's night-work."

The qualities of the Dickinson word rest in the naming. They are themselves, and the frame, or scene is not needed. Dickinsonians have noted my appropriation of Robert Weisbuch's conception of the "scenelessness" of Dickinson's analogies. While Weisbuch points toward an inferred theory of symbolism and my purpose is far more modest, this passage captures something of what I see in the letters as well as the poems: "[Her] scenes are not mimetic but illustratory, chosen, temporary, analogous. The poem is finally sceneless, and this scenelessness is the fully unique quality which identifies Dickinson's lyric technique." In contrast to Dickinson, Weisbuch sets Milton's "Lycidas," a poem in which "a certain state of affairs serves as a goad to to reflective speech," even where "[w]e may value the expression of the mediated situation far more than the motivating situation itself." Dickinson's created scenes are often more significant than the human scenes which gave rise to them. The notion that Dickinson presents "'chance' choices from an infinity of possible exemplifications of [a] poem's unifying proposition" (16) is to me suggestive evidence of Dickinson's wealth of words whose power can establish an important idea about the world. It is as if Dickinson can pierce to essences with any particular instance of the rush of words which occur to her.

In the discussion that led me to think about my version of the "sceneless scene," E. Miller Budick takes that term in a direction different from Weisbuch's notion of Dickinson's analogical bent when she suggests that "Dickinson may be forcing our attention away from parallelisms or analogies, however abstract and absent, and toward the awesome, gaping abyss at the center of phenomenal and noumenal reality both, the abyss that no symbol can bridge but that a multiplicity of false symbols can unwittingly widen" (Budick, 36). Budick develops an interesting set of assertions about Dickinson's manipulations of word-as-symbol, arguing that for her the action of symbol is to "bracket" experience into "phenomenal units," that is separated units of what we see without the overt assertion of how these units form unities (38). Budick goes on to argue that the "sceneless scenes" Dickinson has detached from the contexts of human experience can supplant, with their own life, the experiences from which they rise and the truths toward which they point (41).

My counter-example of Emerson insisted, in Uriel's "sentiment divine / Against the being of a line" that units must be respected, but only because they are structured on the principle that structures unity:

> Line in nature is not found;
> Unit and universe are round;
> In vain produced, all rays return;
> Evil will bless, and ice will burn. (21-25)

Dickinson does not insist on any such thing. Language and meaning focus rather than radiate. Dickinson's ideas about language are not subdued to *use*. In poem 210, language and what it does seem are nearly indistinguishable:

> The thought beneath so light a film—
> Is more distinctly seen
> As laces just reveal the surge—
> Or mists the—Appenine—[sic]

The "film" of language, the figure of speech, evokes the experience, the sight, the emotion instead of processing or developing it in the service of an ulterior assertion, as in "Uriel," or an ulterior scene of service, as in Emerson's meditation on the "match" of words and things. The "celestial veil" converts context into an autonomous, "sceneless scene."

The poem that follows "The thought beneath . . ." in packet 37 acts out these dramatic possibilities:

> Come slowly—Eden!
> Lips unused to Thee—
> Bashful—sip thy Jessamines—
> As the fainting Bee—
>
> Reaching late his flower,
> Round her chamber hums—
> Counts his nectars—
> Enters and is lost in balms

The "thought" veiled beneath these words is not something the words are "in behalf of." Whether the master-tone is set by the theological associations of Eden or by the naturalistic illustration of the bee overcome by sensual fulfillment is not something the poem declares. The "thought" is simply the feeling of being "lost in balms." Whether the Eden is in an Amherst garden or the depths of religious perception is business the poem does not overtly interest itself in.

In his account of the experiences that led him to construct his poems around lines from Dickinson's letters, Turco uses a phrase derived from Donald Davie—abstract syntax—to describe the language-events from which he drew much of his inspiration. His assertion is pretty close to mine: "What one is doing with words when one employs abstract syntax is manipulating connotations, associations, and overtones, not primary meanings, denotations (*The Public Poet*, 30). Denotations would propel us into transactions, either assertions or social contexts. The place of abstract syntax in Dickinson's letters raises another issue, since letters are transactions, transactions which occur in a social context.

What Dickinson does is captured in the letter to her sister-in-law that Stonum quoted (letter 583):

> Cherish Power—dear—
> Remember that stands in the Bible between
>   the Kingdom and the Glory,
> because it is wilder than either of them.

The strains at work between Susan Gilbert Dickinson and her sister-in-law seem to have been serious enough even at the time of this letter to make the word "dear" resonate.[9] Dickinson chose neither the social "kingdom" Susan seems to have inhabited in Amherst, nor the glory—deserved or not—that reflected on her for her mastery of that social world. It is interesting to speculate on what underlay such a letter from Dickinson to the girlhood friend whose intellect struck all who met her. What "wild" power did she think Susan had abjured to live in the kingdom, and bask in glory?

Two letters Dickinson wrote her sister-in-law after the death of her young nephew Gilbert in 1883 illustrate not only the Dickinson way with words, but also the difficulty that power created for her:

> Dear Sue—
>   The Vision of Immortal Life has been fulfilled
>   How simply at the last the Fathom comes! The Passenger and not the sea, we find surprises us—
>   Gilbert rejoiced in Secrets—
>   His Life was panting with them—With what menace of Light he cried "Dont tell, Aunt Emily"! Now my ascended Playmate must instruct me. Show us, prattling Preceptor, but the way to thee!
>   He knew no niggard moment—his life was full of Boon—The Playthings of the Dervish were not so wild as his—

No crescent was this Creature—He traveled from the Full

Such soar, but never set—

I see him in the Star, and meet his sweet velocity in everything that flies—His Life was like the Bugle, which winds itself away, his Elegy an echo—his Requiem ecstasy—

Dawn and meridian in one.

Wherefore would he wait, wronged only of Night, which he left for us—

Without a speculation, our little Ajax spans the whole—

Pass to thy Rendezvous of Light,
Pangless except for us—
Who slowly ford the Mystery
Which thou has leaped across!

Emily (letter 868)

The qualities of scenelessness and an apparently random multiplicity of scenes with only implicit connections between them that Weisbuch and Budick identify with the verse take over in this letter, where the contexts of situation and communicative service are barely maintained, until the resolution into the last four lines, written as verse. In a subsequent letter, the sheer power of abstract syntax seems to me to overwhelm the contexts which, in the examples from Dickinson's youth, her words served so deftly and effectively:

Dear Sue—

A Promise is firmer than a Hope, although it does not hold so much—

Hope never knew Horizon—

Awe is the first Hand that is held to us—

Hopelessness in it's first Film has not leave to last—
That would close the Spirit, and no intercession could do that—

Intimacy with Mystery, after great Space, will usurp
it's [sic] place—
Moving on in the Dark like Loaded Boats at Night,
though there is no Course, there is Boundlessness—

> Expanse cannot be lost—
> Not Joy, but a Decree
> Is Deity—
> His Scene, Infinity—
> Whose rumor's Gate was shut so tight
> Before my Beam was sown,
> Not even a Prognostic's push
> Could make a Dent thereon
>
> The World that thou hast opened
> Shuts for thee,
> But not alone,
> We all have followed thee—
> Escape more slowly
> To thy Tracts of Sheen—
> The Tent is listening,
> But the Troops are gone!

Emily (letter 871)

Here the context of communication to Sue seems to me to
have held more firmly in the prose. What she wrote as verse is
a series of little fragments which act out what Budick saw as
the darker potentiality of Dickinson's symbol-making: "As a
self-ordained, self-contained bit of separable meaning, the
symbol verges on becoming not an avenue of intercourse
among different spheres of existence, not even an "asterisk" or
"sign" pointing in a new direction, but rather a closed-off,
dead fragment of a once larger, once vital meaning" (Budick,
41).

Both letters strive toward verse, in their rushes of effort to
achieve what so effortlessly she had done forty-two and thirty-
one years earlier—color a scene, speak to someone else

through her words of power at a time when such words needed, both for herself and for Susan, to minister. But the probing for essences would not stop in the letters; the movement toward abstraction in syntax was something she could no longer resist or control. It seems to me that in a strange way, words failed her just because of their power. The "Apennine" was too stark, the "heave" of emotion too powerful. Words which, in the language of poem 675, are screws that press essences "out of ordinary meanings," cannot act when the ordinary is so intense.

The problem of abstract syntax, or "words of power" in communicative rather than expressive discourse is for me imaged in a letter of 1881 to Mrs. J.G. Holland, in which she told the story of "[a] Little Boy [who] ran away from Amherst a few Days ago, and when asked where he was going, replied, 'Vermont or Asia.' Many of us go farther" (letter 685). Dickinson's words took her to Asia or beyond, and as her life advanced took her to thoughts, images, and pictures which pierced beyond the world of contexts, whether of systematic thought or social obligation. At times she was the victim of that power, propelled to Asia or beyond when Vermont was what was needed. Richard Sewall notes the penchant for drama and excess in the Dickinsons' family rhetoric, a penchant which seems to have baffled many around them and at times bewildered the family itself. But as the moments of power in Dickinson's letters demonstrate, even in letters which seem not fully to succeed in their response to those exterior occasions which called them into being, Dickinson's power to summon up that drama continues to put into profile for readers the Apennines and the Berkshires, the chickens and that strange listening tent in the 1883 letter to Susan Gilbert Dickinson.

## References

Budick, E. Miller. *Emily Dickinson and the Life of Language: A Study in Symbolic Poetics*. Baton Rouge: Louisiana State Univ. Press, 1985.

Dickinson, Emily. *The Letters of Emily Dickinson*, ed. Thomas H. Johnson and Theodora Ward. 3 vols. Cambridge, MA: Harvard Univ. Press, 1958.

———. *The Poems of Emily Dickinson: Including variant readings*, ed. Thomas H. Johnson. Cambridge, MA: Harvard Univ. Press, 1955.

Emerson, Ralph Waldo. *The Collected Works of Ralph Waldo Emerson*, ed. Alfred R. Ferguson, Joseph Slater, *et al.* 4 vols. to date. Cambridge, MA: Harvard Univ. Press, 1971- .

———. *The Journals and Miscellaneous Notebooks of Ralph Waldo Emerson*, ed. William Gilman, R. H. Orth, *et al.* 16 vol. Cambridge, MA: Harvard Univ. Press, 1960-82.

———. *The Poetry Notebooks of Ralph Waldo Emerson*, ed. Ralph H. Orth, Albert Von Frank, Linda Allardt, and David Hill. Columbia: Univ. of Missouri Press, 1986.

———. *The Complete Works of Ralph Waldo Emerson*, ed. Edward Waldo Emerson. Centenary ed. 12 vols. Boston: Houghton Mifflin, 1903-04.

Sewall, Richard B. *The Life of Emily Dickinson*. 2 vols. New York: Farrar, Straus and Giroux, 1974.

Stonum, Gary Lee. *The Dickinson Sublime*. Madison: Univ. of Wisconsin Press, 1990.

Turco, Lewis. *The New Book of Forms: A Handbook of Poetics*. Hanover, NH: University Press of New England, 1986.

———. *The Public Poet: Five Lectures on the Art and Craft of Poetry*. Ashland, Ohio: Ashland Poetry Press, 1991.

Weisbuch, Robert. *Emily Dickinson's Poetry*. Chicago: Univ. of Chicago Press, 1975.

## Notes

1. Letters are cited by letter number, as assigned in the Johnson edition.

2. See Stonum, chapter 1 for a parallel statement of this issue.

3. I use the text Johnson printed; the other 1862 version is not significantly different; the 1864 and 1883 variants are different kinds of poems entirely.

4. An important word for Emerson—born with, congenitally related.

5. What is most striking about the poem is the fact that it, like the snow-storm of 29 December 1833, seemed "the mad wind's night-work." Emerson recorded it—close to verbatim—in two prose paragraphs in pencil in Notebook 1833. See *PN* 918 and *JMN* 6:246.

6. She revised one of the echoes into the poem during 1862, substituting "Artisans" for "Myrmidons" as she revised the swans out of the version Johnson printed.

7. The spelling of "vail" and Dickinson's immersion in Shakespeare during 1862 makes the phrase "Celestia, Vail" evocative of some archaic usages, such as "vail" as reward or profit, or the setting of the sun, or doing homage to. The earlier version which Johnson did not use as copy-text makes the simpler meaning much more likely: "It flings a Crystal Vail / On Stump—and Stack and Stem—" (12-13).

8. I quote the 1864 version; the 1883 copy was sent to Thomas Niles of Roberts Brothers, with the title "Snow."

9. The entire series of 1878 notes to Susan (letters 580-87) suggest that there was indeed a transaction at work in letter 583, although the content and nuances of that transaction are hard to capture.

MARTA WERNER

# The *Shot Bird's Progress:*
# *Emily Dickinson's* Master Letters

If you saw a bullet
hit a Bird—and he told you
he wasn't shot—you might weep
at his courtesy, but you would
certainly doubt his word—

I

Like all stories, the story of *The Master Letters* is "constructed over a loss."[1] Written in the late 1850s and the early 1860s, when long acquaintance with anonymity first dared Emily Dickinson to test freedom, they were not unsealed again until death blew open the door of her study on 15 May 1886. Hidden, even as her own muse had been cloaked for more than two decades, they were sequestered also from the New England custom of burning the correspondence of the dead, and, for a while, from the interests of editors, biographers, critics. To this date no evidence exists to confirm that these three letters, written on loose sheets of stationery in pencil and in ink, often heavily marked and revised, were ever posted, and the identity of the "Master" remains an enigma. Reciprocity—if it exists at all—is dangerously contrapuntal.

## II

A poet, a fugitive, a woman alone, she must be traced to the doorstep of her Master, "married" to the one man who holds the key to her fleet identity. And this pursuit, charted through study after study of Dickinson's life and poetry, has blinded us all to the extraordinary risks she was then taking with language, to her transgression of genre boundaries, to her re-ordering of form in such a way that the linearity of language itself is deliberately breached and, like the silent fall of the bird with the force of gravity, becomes vertical. Far from being pleading missives misdirected, these letters are poems aimed into inevitability. Here, voice is "an axe shrill singing in the woods."[2] And each fall of the blade, each black mark in the writing tablet leaves an open space, a blank or a light in the spirit. On her way to the "untried country" of imagination she must be stopped. She must be apprehended, encircled. She eludes us, strikes out alone.

## III

"If you saw a bullet / hit a Bird—" The third letter-poem, probably written sometime in 1861, explores and explodes the coordinates of mastery. Forever unfinished, it is a fragment that reveals the ambiguity of desire's progress while also withholding the eschatological moment of salvation. But Dickinson began her letter with an old image of subjection, with the downward flight of a bird remembered perhaps from the works of Elizabeth Barrett Browning or Charlotte Bronte. To draw beyond this beginning, to escape the melody of this fall, she needed to de-create the image and to redefine the boundaries of the self. For once, history acted in complicity with her. When in the nineteenth century the rule of Chance eclipsed the judgment of God, words refused to move towards a center. In the diaspora that followed, all signs were misleading, all final referents forsaken. Lost in the midst of the plotted text where temporality and causality are mere sham, Dickinson chose to wander within the heresy of endlessness.


## IV


—To come nearer
Than Presbyteries—and nearer than
the new coat—that the Tailor
made—the prank of the Heart
at play on the heart—in holy
Holiday—is forbidden me—


Forgetful of redemption, crossing precariously outside the protection of the Master/Logos, Dickinson's cry for union always enfolds the anguished recognition of separateness. Waking in the night to "misgiving," love's suppliant must still plead for severance, purity of purpose, charged silence. . . . These letters, fragments of letters, lay unsent, for no "Master" could have answered them. Called to from out of the empty spaces of vocation, the voice staggers and sings an account of image's transfiguration: "Bird" becoming "Breath" becoming "Queen," "Heart," "Volcano," and finally the force of "No Bird—". Who is "Master" here but the cipher playing inside decipher, the stranger progress of negativity?

Dickinson's letter-poem words itself at a crossroads.

At this instant, "times cross . . . [and] our usual apprehension of successive past and future is translated into another order of time."[3]

At this instant, when one may travel in any direction, "the gap between desire and act is wide. . . . [One is] 'at strife' with [oneself]," mastery is momentarily suspended.[4] Within this gap, this tear, the shot bird makes its return as "No Bird": "No Bird—yet rode in Ether—". Freed from particularity into particles, facing or mirroring openness, Dickinson's "No Bird" sings like Yeats' golden bird "out of nature" and within pure being. Born in the throes of crisis, it sings time struck through with positive silence; it illuminates the "impossible pain and joy" that Simone Weil called poetry.[5]

## VI

In *The Master Letters* there can be no regathering of words into the Word: words are scattered beyond grammar's recollection, words are crumbs strewn at random in a forest—unfollowable. And yet, crisis itself has consecrated them: "These things are [reverent] holy, Sir / I touch them [reverently] hallowed." At last, the letters abolish all forms of mediation: instead of patrilineal enlightenment, the eye of the Master reading, there is a single voice released as a medium for the transmission of light waves and radiant energy. Though one cannot "tell all"— the beginning and the end, the alpha and omega—one can flee through the shards of language towards transfiguration and the truth not of transcendence, but of indeterminacy. And at the crossroads, there is a trace of the holy: "No Bird" flung into the Pleiades, into a pure burning in ether.

## VII

Years of intellectual isolation allowed Dickinson a freedom of speculation greater even than Hester Prynne's. Near the end of her life, she abandoned the sequences of force for a new vertical order, an order outside the linear, printer's logic of the page and beyond the horizon of history. In the 1870s and 1880s the leaves of the folios lay scattered like old love letters. And though these rare and oracular utterances were written in guarded privacy, spoken out of the "hiding places of woman's power," they are no longer in any way private.[6] What speaks in them speaks only after light has broken "into the small house of our cautionary being," after the conditions for inwardness have been reversed.[7] In *The Master Letters*, the fallen bird ascends as "No Bird" to approach the elaborating point of infinity.

## VIII

Tropes of conversion. The hushed silence of Dickinson's will concerning the fate of these letters suggests that she had already turned away from them and entrusted her words to the lyric forces of chance. The anonymity she had suffered during her lifetime was revealed after her death as a mark of good fortune: Unbidden and unread at the time of their writing, *The Master Letters* must now be opened by us. They await an answer. An answer outside the dimensions of power, an answer in the tear.

## IX

"Unlike birds, books die with wings spread open."

Edmond Jabès, *The Book of Dialogue*

## X

No Rose, yet felt myself
a'bloom,
No Bird—yet rode in Ether—

Emily Dickinson, *The Master Letters*

## Notes

My indebtedness to Susan Howe's *My Emily Dickinson* is itself endless. All quotations from Emily Dickinson's letters are taken from *The Master Letters of Emily Dickinson*, edited by Ralph W. Franklin (Amherst: Amherst College Press, 1986).

1. J. Hillis Miller, *Fiction and Repetition* (Cambridge: Harvard University Press, 1982), 61.

2. Emily Dickinson, "An altered look about the hills—," *The Poems of Emily Dickinson*, ed. by Thomas H. Johnson (Cambridge: Harvard University Press, 1955), 99.

3. Frank Kermode, *The Sense of an Ending* (Oxford: Oxford University Press, 1966), 84.

4. Ibid.

5. Simone Weil, *Gravity and Grace*, trans. by Arthur Wills (New York: G. P. Putnam's Sons, 1952), 206.

6. Irene Tayler, *Holy Ghosts* (New York: Columbia University Press, 1990), 300.

7. George Steiner, *Real Presences* (Chicago: The University of Chicago Press, 1989), 143.

# Index of Poetry Titles and First Lines

# General Index

## C

Capps, Jack L., *Emily Dickinson's Reading, 1836-1886*, 123
Chase, Richard, 91; *Emily Dickinson*, 97
"Cherish Power—dear—," 141
Civil War, 89, 126
"Come slowly—Eden," 140
*Commentaries on the Laws of England*, 89
*Compleat Melancholick, The*, 2, 8
*Complete Poems*, 5, 7
*Collected Works of Ralph Waldo Emerson*, 145; *Complete Works of Ralph Waldo Emerson*, 145
connate, 133, 134, 146 (definition)
connotations, 140
context, 140, 142, 144
"Crimson Children," 2
Crowell, Mary Warner, 128
cryptogram, 91

## D

"Dainty Sum, A," 6
Davie, Donald, abstract syntax, 2-3, 4-5, 140; dramatic syntax, 4; *Articulate Energy*, 7; objective syntax, 4; subjective syntax, 4
denotations, 140
Derrida, Jacques, *Spurs*, 95
*Desire in Language*, 95
Dickinson, Austin, 99, 103, 105-106, 107, 121, 125-126, 129, 130-133
Dickinson, Edward, 31, 66, 89, 91-95, 97, 106, 131-132
Dickinson, Emily, *Complete Poems*, 5, 7, 94, 123; *Bolts of Melody: New Poems*, 7; *Letters*, ed. Mabel Loomis Todd, 5, 7; *Poems [First Series]*, 8; *Poems, Second Series*, 8; *Poems, Third Series*, 8; letters nos. 42, pp. 131-133, 137; 110, p. 106; 117, p. 119; 177, p. 105; 208, p. 119 (see also poem 222); "Master Letter" no. 187, pp. 124, 147 *ff.*; 208, p. 120 (see also poem 218); "Master Letter" no. 233, pp. 124, 147 *ff.*; "Master Letter" no. 248, pp. 124, 147 *ff.*; 261, p. 91; 277, p. 119; 342b, p. 91; 411, p. 119; 430, pp. 107, 124; 531, p. 121 (see also poem 1401); 581, p. 107; 583, pp. 130-132, 141, "Cherish Power—dear—," 141; 584, p. 102; 685, p. 144; 735, p. 119 (see also poem 1512); 757, p. 101; 854, p. 102; 908, p. 101; 868, pp. 141-142; 871, pp. 142-143; 912, "Morning might come by accident, Sister," pp. 119-121; 921, "Morning," pp. 100, 102, 115-117, 119-121, 121-122; 975, p. 120 (see also poem 1637); 999, p. 107; "Master Letters," nos. 187, 233, 248, "If you saw a bullet," pp. 124, 147 *ff.*, 151-2; *The Manuscript Books*, 94, 123, 127; no. 37, p. 140; Journal, 187, 252, 341, 376, 512, 792, 1760, p. 96; "Of Course I

Prayed," 96; poems nos. 4, p. 111; 14, p. 111; 27, "Morns like these—we parted—," p. 109; 96, p. 125; 106, p. 125; 210, "The thought beneath so light a film," pp. 139-140; 211, "Come slowly—Eden," 140; 216, p. 127; 218, p. 120 (see also letter 232); 222, p. 120 (see also letter 208); 246, p. 125; 296, p. 125; 300, "'Morning'—means 'Milking'," p. 115; 311, "It sifts from leaden sieves," pp. 133-135; 336, p. 125; 366, p. 125; 446, p. 125; 461, p. 125; 494, p. 125; 501, "This World is not Conclusion," p. 137; 673, "'Tis This—invites—appalls—," pp. 112-113; 675, p. 144; 680, "Ungained—it may," 113; 696, p. 110; 809, p. 110; 382, "Escape from Circumstances," p. 111; 1208, "Our own/possessions—," pp. 113-114; 1209, p. 133; 1248, p. 105; 1260, p. 110; 1401, p. 123 (see also letter 531); 1454, p. 117; 1488, "Birthday of," p. 114; 1512, "It is solemn to remember that Vastness," p. 119 (see also letter 735); 1515, "The things that never can come back," p. 120; 1637, p. 120 (see also letter 975); 1719, p. 110; "Safe in Their Alabaster Chambers," 106-7; "Snow," 146; *The Single Hound: Poems of a Lifetime* by Emily

Dickinson, ed. Martha Dickinson Bianchi, 108, 127; *The Master Letters of Emily Dickinson*, ed. Franklin, Ralph W., 124, 151; lexicon, 128; packet [manuscript book] 37, 141; *The Letters of Emily Dickinson*, ed. Thomas H. Johnson and Theodora Ward, 145; 146, notes 6-9
Dickinson, Emily Norcross, 78, 91-94, 95, 132
Dickinson, Gilbert, 103, 107, 121, 141-142
Dickinson, Lavinia, 109, 127, 131-132
Dickinson, Martha—see Bianchi, Martha Dickinson
Dickinson, Susan Huntington Gilbert, 99 *ff.*; 130-131, 141-144
*Dickinson Sublime, The*, 145
*Dickinson: The Anxiety of Gender*, 103
discourse, 93, 137
dramatic syntax, 4

E

"Ear of Silence, The," 2
echolalia, 95
Eliot, T. S., *The Waste Land*, 3, 8
Emerson, Ralph Waldo, 128, 129, 133 *ff.*; "The Snow Storm," 133-135; *Journals and Miscellaneous Notebooks*, 135, 145, 146; *Poetry Notebooks*, 145, 146; no. 1833, p. 146; *Collected Works*, 145; *Complete Works*, 145; "The Poet," 136; "Uriel," 139-140, 146

Dickinson's Language as Autonomous Action," 129 ff.

ACO 3331                           9/7/93

PS
3570
U626
E45
1993

0 00 02 0579358 1
MIDDLEBURY COLLEGE